This book is due for return on or before the date last
stamped below unless an extension of time is granted

-9. JAN. 1969	1 2 DEC 2005	
23. JAN. 1969	1 2 OCT 2011	
15. FEB. 1971		
-9. MAR. 1971		
-1. APR. 1971		
25. NOV 1980		
31. MAR 1981		
10. FEB. 1993		
-3 APR 1995		
3 0 OCT 1995		
2 8 FEB 2002		
-3 FEB 2004		
3 1 OCT 2005		
2 3 NOV 2005		

(P.1642)

TRAMPOLINING:
A Complete Handbook

TRAMPOLINING:
A Complete Handbook

DENNIS E. HORNE

FABER AND FABER
24 Russell Square
London

First published in mcmlxviii
by Faber and Faber Limited
24 Russell Square London WC1
Printed in Great Britain by
Latimer Trend & Co Ltd Plymouth
All rights reserved

SBN 571 08471 0

⧫ 7210

I dedicate this book to
TED BLAKE
Without his early appreciation
of the contribution the trampoline
could make to the physical education
programme and the way in which he
has devoted many years in leading
its development throughout the world,
this book would never
have been written

Author's Preface

Throughout my travels and communications with many people interested in trampolining, there has always been an atmosphere about the 'layman' of being 'lost' in the world of Rebound Tumbling. The thirst for knowledge of this new sport has never been satisfactorily quenched. Very few books have been written on this subject and of those which have been written, the majority are of American origin. This, perhaps, is very natural since the sport originated and was used both recreationally and competitively for thirteen years before we, in Britain, had the opportunity to appreciate its values. Now, Britain rates very high in the world of trampolining and, therefore, it is about time we made some sort of contribution on the technical side as well as on the practical side.

The importance of the trampoline as a piece of educational apparatus has successfully passed through the 'teething stages' and is now readily accepted by educational authorities, medical establishments, and the military services. Trampolines have been installed in universities and physical educational colleges across the whole of the Continent and Europe and as far apart as London and Sydney. Educational committees throughout Britain automatically purchase this apparatus as an essential piece of equipment in new schools. Even the governors of special schools for physically and mentally handicapped children have realized that the trampoline has a great deal to offer to these less fortunate children. During the Second World War, the American air crews used the trampoline for part of their training. This activity requires co-ordination, balance, aerial orientation and control. Today, many of the military services of the world train their men with the aid of the trampoline.

Hundreds of physical education teachers, coaches and performers are entering into the realms of this new sport each year; all these people are seeking the 'know-how' of this activity so that they may further their own knowledge and impart this on to others. It is with these people in mind that I have decided to compile this book to aid them in their work.

I do not profess that this book will be the answer to all our problems; in fact, if there were no problems there would be no progress, and our sport would be far less interesting. I do hope, however, that the book will enable both coach and performer to glean much information to fill many of the unanswered gaps in their knowledge of the sport and move on to a successful and happy time in the sphere of trampolining.

Contents

Illustrations

ILLUSTRATIONS

Introduction

It is very difficult, even impossible I would say, to put a date to the origin of rebound tumbling. It could be said that it began with the birth of the human being. For along with running, climbing and swimming, jumping has always been one of our natural activities. I am sure that the very early human must have found some springy surface from which to jump. The most common piece of rebound tumbling equipment, and our first introduction to this form of activity, has usually been the nursery bed! Children have bounced, dived, rolled and tumbled from the time they began to walk. When people took to entertaining themselves and others of their community, various devices were improvised to create interest. It was found that a plank of wood raised from the ground provided a wonderful surface from which to leap high into the air. Amongst the travelling acrobatic entertainers of the Middle Ages, there were people who specialized in this type of performance, and would jump and spring over various obstructions and even over each other. Everyone, I would say, has at one time or another taken part in that very popular camping activity of being 'tossed in the blanket'. If you have never been forced to give an exhibition of your aerial gyroscopics, I am sure you are guilty of adding your energy to the impetus of that poor defenceless flyer. From the wastelands of the Antarctic, we have heard that even the Eskimos stretch walrus skins between stakes in the ice and jump up and down on them for recreation and amusement. Who knows, perhaps, one day we may see them perform at the World Trampolining Championships.

The first record we have of a specially manufactured piece of

15

apparatus for this sport dates back to 1936. An American diving and tumbling champion, by the name of George Nissen, was also a great lover of circus acrobats and whenever he had the opportunity he would follow the circus to town. One thing which always enthralled him was the way the trapeze artist ended his act by dropping onto his safety-net and performed intricate movements on the rebound. Whilst watching this type of performance one day, he realized that here was something that was exciting in its own right; exciting to watch and exciting to perform. Motivated by his thoughts, George set about constructing a prototype model from scrap metal he had collected around the neighbourhood. His workshop in those early days was his father's garage in Cedar Rapids, Iowa. He called the result of his work his 'T' Model'. The 'T' stood for the word Trampoline. George chose the word from a combination of circus terms he had learned: there was the Italian 'Trampoli', which meant 'performing on stilts'; the Spanish 'Trampolin', which was the name given to the Teta-board or spring-board. It is even said that there was a French trapeze artist by the name of Du Trampoline who was noted for his rebound work at the end of his performance. George Nissen put a great deal of thought into his planning of a standard type of trampoline. It had to be of a size where it could be placed easily into a workable space and at the same time be large enough to be a safe piece of apparatus. It had to have sufficient height from the floor so that even the heaviest of jumpers did not stretch the suspension system so far as to allow him to hit the ground whilst performing. The apparatus had to be heavy and strong enough to remain anchored to the ground during continual bombardment and yet light enough to be transportable by children.

Throughout the Second World War, the American Armed Forces adopted the trampoline as part of their training. The flyers, in particular, were able to experience aerial orientation, and at the same time, develop all round skill and co-ordination; a very important factor in modern warfare. Like so many things it takes a war to enable drastic new developments to take place; this also seemed to be the case with trampolining. Maybe because of its adoption by the forces or because more people were

16

able to experience its values, the trampoline did not die with the end of the war. Together with a number of the top physical educationalists in the U.S.A., George Nissen set about developing trampolining as a sport in its own right. Courses and demonstrations were arranged, programmes planned, instructional films, check-off lists, wall charts and articles published.

Jumping is a spontaneous and natural activity necessary for the growth and development of a young body and mind and, therefore, it plays an integral part in any physical education programme. Introduce rebound tumbling into the school physical educational programme, the youth club or even your own back garden and a child's natural interest is immediately aroused. The need to encourage them to jump will be non-existent; the main difficulty will be trying to stop them! There is just something about a trampoline which fascinates both young and old. This interest and enthusiasm in trampolining is often a means of drawing new members to clubs as well as preparing new blood for other activities such as gymnastics and diving since the aerial gyrations performed on the trampoline carry over very easily to these other sports. The trampoline offers the opportunity to develop all-round skill and co-ordination by subjecting its pupils to a wide range of combination and repetitive movement situations besides developing the cardio-respiratory systems in a most enjoyable manner. With other similar activities, i.e. diving, tumbling and gymnastics, there are certain restrictions to the range of movements. The take-offs and landings may only be from, and to, the feet or hands. With trampolining, many other parts of the body can be used, thereby extending the range and complexity of possible movements. This greater range of movement allows for any type of person, large or small, strong or weak, daring or timid, to meet with a certain amount of success right from the very first sensation of bouncing up and down. Blind and handicapped children have derived a great deal of benefit from its springy bed, so much so that doctors and specialists are amongst its most ardent supporters—but more on this subject in a special chapter later in the book. It is also a most suitable activity for the whole family irrespective of sex or age. Children have mastered the four basic drops as early as $3\frac{1}{2}$ years

B   17

of age and youngsters of 70 years have turned to this thrilling exercise as a new challenge, learning and mastering somersaults and still wanting to learn more. Should anyone wish to go to the top of this exhilarating sport the scope is unending. There is no fear of mastering all it has to offer since the individual movements that can be performed are unbelievable and the different combinations go on *ad infinitum*, There is no other sport which covers such an active age range. Because this activity is so enjoyable and allows an individual to work at his own level, although still enticing him to reach out for new experiences, there is never a lack of enthusiasm.

In the U.S.A. the first unofficial National Championship was held during the Amateur Athletic Union Championships in 1947. This event was won by a young fellow named James Garner. It is recorded that Jimmy's coach, George Paul, was the first person to perform triple twisting somersaults way back in 1932. In 1948 the National Collegiate Athletic Association accepted rebound tumbling as a regular event at their National Collegiate Gymnastic Competitions, but so far as the A.A.U. was concerned, trampolining continued as an unofficial event in the United States for seven long years until 1954. The pioneer champions during those early years were Robert Schoendube in 1948 and Edsel Buchanan in 1949 and 1950. There was a break for one year in 1951 when no contest was held. In 1952 Frank LaDue came on the scene, winning the title and then later doing much fine work in really establishing trampolining as a new sport. 1953 saw the last of the unofficial champions in Richard Gutting and, at long last, in 1954, the American Athletic Union accepted trampolining as an official competitive event with Robert Elliot making history by having his name placed in the official records as the first National Trampoline Champion of the U.S.A. This was the first step on the ladder to success and George Nissen's contribution to the world of sport. The following year trampolining took its place in the Pan-American Games in Mexico City. Getting into the 'Games' Series was certainly a big step and negotiations were started to include it in the other National and World Games.

The rules for competition routines also underwent a great

proving time until the present set of rules was thought to be the most suitable. Originally a performer was allowed 45 seconds in which to show what movements he could execute during one routine, based on a similar idea used for the floor exercises in Olympic Gymnastics. It was soon found that 45 seconds was a very long time to allow for a competition routine and so the ruling was changed and a definite number of contacts with the bed was introduced. The new ruling required three eight-bounce routines with a resting period of 10 seconds between each routine. Again the rules were adjusted so that the competitors only had to perform two routines, but these were lengthened to ten bounces and the resting period to 20 seconds. To allow for greater scope the Americans' present system has evolved to one routine consisting of anything from ten to twelve contacts with the bed. It was just prior to this final decision by the Americans that Great Britain and the European countries began holding their own competitions. Reflecting over the greater experience of the Americans in organizing competitions of this nature, we and the European countries used the two-routine system as had been used in the United States. There was, however, a slight difference, which was to make both routines a series of eight bounces and one of the routines a compulsory set exercise.

In 1957 George and Annie Nissen, Ted Blake, Frank LaDue (All-American Diving and Trampolining Champion) and Kurt Baechler, a very keen trampolinist from Switzerland, travelled many thousands of miles to make the sport of trampolining known to other parts of Britain, the Continent and Europe. Following the initial impact, Kurt stayed on in Europe to continue the good work. Now and again Frank would return and together they won over the physical educationists of the different countries. After three years of giving demonstrations, lectures, running courses and generally selling a great activity, their tremendous drive and enthusiasm for this sport became contagious and trampolining well and truly caught on and developed at a fantastic rate. Others became disciples of these men and they in turn became leaders in their own right. Among them were Dr. Heinz Braeklein who became Bundesobmann for trampolining in the Deutsches Turnerbund; Professor Frank Matthys, Commissioner for Sports at the University of Brussels; The Federal School of Sport in Magglingen, Switzerland; Hellmut Rohnisch in Sweden; Klass Boot in Holland; Grunde Vegard in Norway; Gustave Kraemer in Denmark. The list became longer and longer every month.

Following their European tour, George, his wife Annie and Frank LaDue travelled farther afield to South Africa, Bermuda, Mexico and Japan. During 1959 they spent several weeks in these countries putting on their spectacular and flawless exhibitions of individual and synchronized bouncing and once again left behind them a trail of enthusiasts determined to put the sport of trampolining to the fore in their country. In Australia, Alan Plowman and Norman Pressey became the pioneers. For New Zealand, the Jack Bonham family took on the responsibility of this task. And in Japan the Senoh Company of Tokyo, later accompanied by Phil Drips, a one time member of the U.S. Navy Trampoline Display Team, began to develop this sport there. South Africa was so captivated by it all that Olle Areborn arranged for another visit by the American Masters of rebound tumbling. The team which made the tour in 1960 included Ed Cole, who was a former Big Ten and National Rebound Tumbling champion as well as being the world professional indoor diving champion (notice once again how the combination of diving and trampolining go together), and Ron Munn—also a National Rebound Tumbling champion. Ron Munn stayed behind in South Africa for two years to help establish a very flourishing association. Always on hand and deserving great credit were Sydney Trimmer and his brother Martin, and Nick Hayes. These dedicated men have created a trampolining nation of very high calibre which must be carefully reckoned with in the future. And so trampolining began to develop throughout the world. Organizations to handle the sport were set up in each country and enthusiasts originated their own national rules, regulations and championships. Much work had to be done but there were always many willing helpers who offered their services to see that this new contribution to sport, rebound tumbling, or trampolining, was given every assistance to succeed. The apparatus sold itself; it just needed organizing.

1

Safety Precautions

Before attempting any new activity, one should be aware of the advantages and disadvantages of this particular activity. So often a new experience is pursued until there comes a time when the person is completely baffled; it is then, and only then, that the performer usually refers to the instructions. Sometimes this is too late and the damage is done; the same could apply to trampolining.

In order to make certain that these safety precautions are easily assimilated and for the purpose of quick reference, I shall classify them in chronological order as follows:

1. Unfolding a trampoline.
2. Safety precautions prior to the use of the trampoline.
3. Safety to the performer during use.
4. Folding a trampoline.
5. Safety precautions after use.
6. Portaging.

1. Unfolding a Trampoline

It is only natural that when a trampoline first arrives on the scene, the immediate reaction is to open it up and start jumping. But firstly, there is a right and a wrong way to unfold a trampoline. The trampoline is divided into three sections, two end pieces and one centre piece.

When viewed in the transporting position it will be noted that the weight of one end piece and one set of legs is used to hold the other end and legs in place. Should this top 'flap' be lifted

21

away unsuspectingly, then the result is a resounding 'clang' as the legs or end pieces on that side collapse to the ground.

Stand facing the side of the trampoline on which the legs are positioned. Take hold of the uppermost leg with one hand and the other leg with the other hand. Release the lower leg by pulling the upper leg towards you and downwards. This will rotate the whole trampoline about the supporting pins on the roller-stands. The lower leg can then be placed onto the floor. Continue rotating the trampoline, pulling the legs still being held, to the fully extended position and place it on the floor. Move round to the other leg and crouch down facing along the long side. Take hold of the roller stand, just above the wheel, with the outer hand and hold the leg below the tension chain with the inner hand. Shuffle backwards lifting the trampoline by the leg so that the weight is on the far leg. This will enable you to extend the leg being held and at the same time pull the roller-stand towards you, allowing the trampoline to stand securely on its own two legs. Repeat this operation on the other side. If the trampoline is not lifted, or the body is not shuffled backwards during this operation, the weight of the trampoline will bear down on the wheels of the roller-stands as they are tilted, forcing them into the body of the performer or pinning him between the roller-stands and legs. This can be very painful!

The trampoline is now standing on its two legs with the end pieces folded to the middle. The top piece is lifted and guided to the vertical position. Move to the other side and support this end piece down to the horizontal position. Should the end piece be allowed to drop down under its own weight it is possible that the hinges will snap or be damaged in some way. There are end braces attached to the end pieces and these are engaged into sleeves attached to the legs. Hold on to the frame and guide these end braces into the sleeves with the foot. The lower the foot is placed on each brace, the more control is in evidence. Repeat the same procedure at the other end.

2. Safety Precautions Prior to the Use of the Trampoline

In a number of cases during this section, I shall be referring to factors which apply to trampolines which have been used many times before rather than brand-new ones, but even so, these items are still worth checking.

Firstly, when siting a trampoline, make sure that there is sufficient height overhead. It can be most disconcerting to a performer about to execute his latest and most complicated movement before an audience to find himself hanging from a chandelier at the top of his height! The types of bed available today range from the solid sheet of nylon to the thin stringmesh. Usually, the finer the mesh of the bed, the higher the performer is able to bounce, but this is not always the case and I am not going into details here. As the standards of the beds and the type of suspension improve, so allowance must be made for the achievement of greater height. At the moment we usually suggest not less than 25 ft. between bed and ceiling. It has been known for trampolining to take place in a hall or gymnasium having the necessary height, but for the trampoline to be situated directly beneath lights, beams, gymnastic apparatus or other suspended hazards! This can quite easily be done where people are enthusiastic to get on with their bouncing quickly.

The roller-stands are sometimes left attached to the frame so that they are not misplaced or because they make a very nice means of stepping on to the trampoline. Other people take them away because they impair the normal supporting procedure. To keep them close to hand, these roller-stands are sometimes placed beneath the trampoline with devastating results. Anyone performing a Seat or Front Drop under these conditions will bear me out! The area beneath the trampoline must be kept absolutely free from any obstruction. Anything falling beneath the bed from the pockets of a performer, or rolling from persons other than the performer, must be left until the bouncer has stopped. To crawl under a trampoline to collect any articles could be disastrous to both bouncer and retriever.

The dress of performers can be of great importance and many minor grazes and discomforts can be avoided by following these few words of advice. For beginners especially, the following articles of clothing, or something similar, should be worn:

23

Long-sleeved jumper. This is very necessary when learning movements involving a Front Drop. During a Front Drop the bone at the elbow is inclined to get in the way. At this point there is no flesh and the skin is sandwiched between this bone and the bed of the trampoline. A certain amount of friction occurs and the skin usually gets broken if not covered. There is nothing more off-putting to a newcomer to the sport than the sight of blood spattered over the bed.

Long gymnastic trousers. The reason for wearing long trousers is similar to that for wearing a long-sleeved jumper except that the points to be protected are the knees instead of the elbows. These trousers should be of the stretch variety so that there is no restriction of movement.

Socks. Now and again the instep of the foot is inclined to get grazed on Front and Knee Drops for the same reasons as above and the socks prevent this from happening.

Soft gymnastic shoes. The tops of the toes can become very sore when learning Front and Knee Drops and when a web bed is being used the toe-nails are sometimes inclined to get torn or broken if they get caught under the webbing; so these shoes, naturally, protect the feet.

Having stated what *should* be worn there are also many articles which *should not* be worn. There are far too many to list them all here and I am sure that even if I tried, I would still miss many of them. Therefore, I will mention only a few of the obvious ones.

Necklaces. Sometimes worn by both girls and boys, they can be dangerous if flicked into the face whilst jumping up and down. They may also get tangled in the webbing on Front Drops, or supporters may catch hold of them in carrying out their duty of stopping performers from falling off the trampoline.

Rings. Can be dangerous if the wearer accidently hits or scratches someone supporting.

Wristwatch. If the glass front smashes and splinters on to the bed and floor the particles are very difficult to find.

Belt buckles. These are inclined to get caught in the webbing of the bed during Front Drops and can cause damage to the bed.

Buttons and metal badges can also catch in the webbing, causing clothing to be torn and ripped.

Basketball boots. Footwear of this nature should definitely be discouraged during bouncing. Since the ankle joint cannot be fully extended whilst wearing a boot, the body is tilted forward in a Knee Drop, causing the performer to pitch forward on to his face or on to the frame of the trampoline. The body cannot compensate by leaning backward because the arch in the back may cause even greater harm, as will be explained fully in the chapter on Basic Movements.

Spectacles. The decision regarding spectacles must be left to the discretion of the wearer. Naturally, where possible it is better that the performer takes them off whilst bouncing, but I know of many performers who cannot see without them and have bounced quite safely while still wearing them. It is possible to purchase a special rubber retainer which is fitted to the frame and extends round the back of the head, gripping the spectacles firmly in place.

Finger-nails. Finger-nails and toe-nails should always be kept short. They can be a source of danger to both the performer and to people supporting around the sides. Nails can catch in the webbing and also the skin.

I have already mentioned the people who stand around the frame of the trampoline acting as supporters and now I am going to explain their duties. The correct name given to these people is 'spotters'. The reason for this name is that they continually watch a certain spot around the performer's body. This spot is also the centre of gravity of the performer. By watching this area (or 'spotting' its position), these spotters are able to determine the direction in which the performer is going to move and, therefore, be prepared to prevent the performer from hurting himself or falling off. These spotters are a most invaluable part of trampolining and should always be in attendance whenever the sport is practised.

The prescribed number of spotters per trampoline is usually not less than four; one to each side. More than this number is, of course, acceptable. As a trampolinist progresses, however, he is more inclined to lean forwards and backwards rather than

sideways. Because of this, should there be a shortage of spotters
—and only for this reason—it is possible for the bouncer to perform having only two spotters, positioned one at each end, but
this should be the absolute minimum. In all national and international competitions there must always be four spotters in
attendance. If the finest performers in the world require this
number, then it is certain that the average bouncer should not
bounce with less.

Fig. 1

All spotters should stand in a position leaning against the
trampoline with one leg braced back. The arms should rest on
the frame with the hands in a position ready to push a performer
back onto the bed (Fig. 1). By watching the region of the performer's centre of gravity, spotters are able to observe the position of the body weight around this point. Should there be an
excess of body weight in front of the centre of gravity then the
performer will travel forward. If there is excess weight behind
the centre of gravity then the performer will move backward.
Being alert to this directional movement enables the spotters to
prepare themselves well in advance of any mishap. When in-
troducing beginners to this sport, I usually explain the support-

ing position of the spotters to all of them, and then whilst they stand around the trampoline in this position, I perform a series of Seat Drops, pushing myself backward towards each of them in turn. By doing this, they each experience the sensation of someone travelling towards them and having to push against this weight in order to prevent an accident. In this way the new spotters can be conditioned gradually, if necessary, to what is expected of them. I have often seen spotters, youngsters especially, uninitiated to this art, run or move away when performers are travelling towards them. If a spotter is not going to stand his ground under all conditions then he should not be there. His action could prevent or cause an accident! Last, but

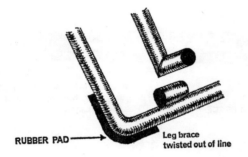

RUBBER PAD ——→   Leg brace
twisted out of line

Fig. 2

by far not the least, is the availability of a first-aid kit at all times.

Now and again children, when left to erect the trampoline by themselves, are in such a great hurry to be the first ones to bounce that the final stages of erection are sometimes omitted, either hoping, or thinking, that someone else will complete the job for them. The most common of these omissions are the end braces. Through use, the Allan nut, holding the brace secure, becomes loose and the arm of the brace is moved out of line to the sleeve in which it engages (Fig. 2). Because this twist stops an easy entry into the sleeve, a child is apt to give up easily and leave it undone. All that is required is for the securing nut to be loosened, the brace twisted and placed into its correct position, and then the nut tightened. At the other end of the brace, where

27

it is attached to the frame, there is also a danger spot (Fig. 3). The large bolt about which the brace swivels, and by which it is anchored to the frame, can work loose through continual bouncing. If this should happen to both braces at one end, this end could catapult upward causing a bouncer great harm. The restraining chains of the legs are also liable to work loose and, therefore, these too should be checked periodically. The chains are attached to the frame by means of a metal collar. This collar is securely held in place by two more Allan nuts. If the tension of these chains is not kept to the correct pitch there will be a tremendous strain on the hinges at that end which in turn can cause even greater damage. Keep that Allan key handy, it is far more valuable than its size implies.

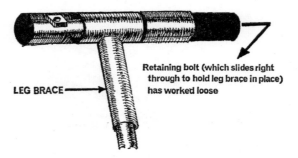

LEG BRACE

Retaining bolt (which slides right through to hold leg brace in place) has worked loose

Fig. 3

Whenever possible fit frame pads to the apparatus since these have a great psychological bearing on the confident way in which a performer bounces, besides giving a certain amount of protection should someone land on the frame. These pads are made from foam rubber or ether foam covered by a vinyl sheeting. Specially shaped clips are attached for easy fitting. For the long sides there are specially-designed pads 18 in. in width which allow a coach to stand on the frame to administer manual support easily. These are called Safe 'T' Sides. A further metal attachment is required since these sides have to be strong enough to carry the weight of a fully-grown man moving along them. The newer models have this attachment automatically

28

welded on as part of the equipment but for the older models one can buy a simple fitting which is well worth the extra cost.

3. Safety to the Performer During Use

Having checked that all the necessary pre-bouncing safety precautions have been observed we can now get down to work. Normally, we only allow one bouncer at a time on the trampoline bed because it is very easy for one performer to land just before the other, causing what is known as a 'kip'. The result of this kip can send the unprepared bouncer high into the air and out of control. The reverse can also happen: by landing immediately after a performer, the bed can be depressed further, taking it away from his body weight at the very moment he expects a strong recoil. Instead of flying high he will then collapse in a heap on the bed. In both these instances a collision between the two performers can very easily occur. Double bouncing (two people performing on the same trampoline) is only used by experienced trampolinists for display work and for relaxation. Being experienced they work well within their capabilities and are prepared for any slight adjustment which may be called for. Sometimes an experienced coach may allow two absolute beginners to learn movements side by side across the bed but on these occasions no preliminary bounces take place. As beginners, the bouncers will only perform the very basic drops in this manner and as these are flat landings there is no chance of a high recoil.

When activities on a trampoline are unsupervised by a responsible person, there will always be someone who will want to act the fool, to the delight of an audience. Horse-play of any kind must be checked immediately before it develops beyond the point of control. Besides the obvious results which happen under any circumstances, the recoiling surface of the trampoline adds impetus to any movement making the results more devastating. Although in the normal way this never happens to many people in charge of classes, now and again something extraordinary does occur. I would like to mention one or two incidents of which I have heard during conversation with various people. At one club, great amusement was gained from throwing bottles and glasses across a trampoline between the bouncer and bed whilst the performer was jumping; and at others in flicking lighted cigarette ends at a person bouncing up and down. It has been known in some schools for small boys to be folded in the middle of a trampoline when it was put away. This will give you some idea of what could happen if supervision was lax and safety precautions were not strictly adhered to. In America, during a census on trampoline accidents, it was discovered that more accidents were caused through people eating, drinking or smoking whilst on a trampoline than by any other means.

A teacher or coach should always insist on a set sequence for mounting and dismounting the trampoline rather than allow a free-for-all when it is time for the next performer to take his turn. There are various ways in which this can be done and the person in charge of the group should adopt whichever method he thinks is the most workable for his particular requirements. The spotters standing around the trampoline may be given a number, which is the cue for that performer to mount the trampoline as soon as his number is called. The spotters could remain in set positions around the frame and as soon as the person to the right or left has finished bouncing then the next take his turn. Some prefer to rotate the spotters around the frame, moving one place to the left or right each time a different performer is required. In this way the mounting and dismounting will always take place at exactly the same position each time. Always make certain that one performer is safely off the trampoline before the other gets on.

There is a correct method for mounting a trampoline as well as for dismounting. When mounting, place both hands on the frame, shoulder-width apart and with the fingers facing towards each other. The elbows should point out sideways. From a push from the floor the body weight should be supported by the hands. One leg should then be placed sideways outside the hands with the foot resting on the frame. This foot is then brought towards the hands and the second foot placed beside it. Having gained balance the body may stand erect. Make certain at this point that the performer steps straight from the frame onto the bed and not between the cables! As confidence and ability increase, the foot may be placed between the hands straight from the initial jump from the floor.

It must be instilled into beginners right from their introduction to trampolining that jumping straight from the bed to the ground is absolutely forbidden. Having become accustomed to the soft landing on the bed, this sudden change to a solid landing could cause injury to both the feet and the spine. The correct method of dismounting is to place one hand and the opposite foot on to the frame, for even distribution of body weight, and then draw the second leg between these two, directing it towards the ground. The body can then be lowered gently onto the ground through this leading foot. There are many different ways in which advanced performers may dismount, such as from back drops, somersaults and twisting somersaults, but I shall not go into the explanations here.

To start a beginner bouncing we usually stand him on the cross in the centre of the bed. His eyes should focus on the end of the red line which bisects the length of the bed and his feet should be placed on either side of this red line, hip-width apart in order to form a wide base for balance purposes. The bodyweight must be distributed evenly over the soles of both feet. By bending the knees and pushing into the bed and at the same time swinging the arms vigorously past the thighs forward and upwards, the bed will be depressed. The resultant recoil will send the performer into the air. A positive way of seeing how the arm swing depresses the bed (Action and Reaction) would be to stand on a set of bathroom scales and swing the arms up above the head. The needle indicating the normal weight would then spin round to a higher reading. When bouncing, the arm action should be similar to that for skipping backward. The arms are kept straight throughout. Each time the performer is about to make contact with the bed, the arms should swing past the thighs so that the upward swing coincides with the bending of the knees and the pushing into the bed. The only time that the arms move behind the line of the body is just before the landing. From the top of the flight the arms swing sideways to a position just behind the seat and then a new cycle commences.

Having set the body in motion it is rather useful to know how it can be stopped! As the feet land, the recoil from the bed is absorbed through the body by bending the knees. It must be remembered that as the bed returns to its normal position the knees will be forcibly bent forwards and upwards. To ensure that the performer is not thrown off balance through this impact, the upper half of the body should lean forward as a counter balance. As soon as a performer finds he is moving towards the edge of the bed, he should immediately check, or 'kill', the bounce as a safety precaution. Practice in 'killing the bounce' should be made compulsory for all beginners before they are allowed to advance to performing stunts.

Too much bouncing during one turn exhausts the body very quickly. Always remember that vertigo and fatigue run together; therefore, keep to short useful turns. Often too much unnecessary bouncing exhausts the performer before he executes any movement. Keep build-up bounces to a minimum. Gradual lead-up stages or progressions are other great safety precautions. Possibly these are the most important of all, for if a performer builds up a complicated movement step by step, never progressing further until absolutely certain that each of these steps has been properly mastered, then there is less chance for an accident to happen. Spotters, although prepared, may never have to move; frame-pads may never be touched; blind, uncontrollable landings may never occur and, what is more, your squad will acquire a great deal of confidence in you and their own performances.

4. Folding a Trampoline

The session is over and fun has been had by everyone. All that remains now is to fold up the trampoline, have a shower, and move on. Rather than tell you to reverse the procedure as mentioned earlier under the heading of 'Unfolding a Trampoline', I am going through each stage of the folding under a separate heading. In this way there will be no confusion, especially as one or two movements are slightly different.

1. Youngsters thoroughly enjoying the fun of trampolining.

2. Queues of people waiting their turn at one of the trampolining parks in America.

3. Annie Nissen demonstrating a forward and backward splits jump.

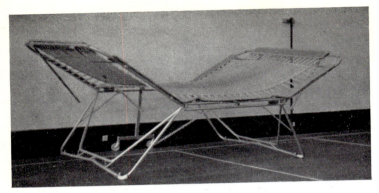

4–8. UNFOLDING A TRAMPOLINE

9–11. UNFOLDING A TRAMPOLINE

12–15. FOLDING A TRAMPOLINE

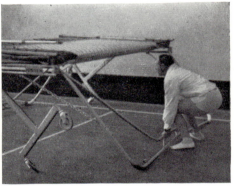

Stand facing the trampoline in line with one set of legs. Take hold of the frame with both hands and place one foot as low on the end brace as possible. Lean away from the trampoline keeping one foot on the end brace and the knee locked. Bend the other knee and swing the body weight under the trampoline. Because the extended leg is kept stiff the body weight travels along the shafts of this leg forcing the brace from the sleeve. Repeat on the other side making sure you keep hold of the frame, otherwise the end piece may catapult upward causing some anxiety. Having raised the end piece to the vertical, move round to the other side to lower it to rest on the frame. Exactly the same procedure should take place to lower the other end. At this point the roller stands should be replaced if they had been removed. Now comes the important decision as to what to do next, and this is where a number of people make the wrong decision. Move round to the end which was last folded. This is easily recognized by the expanse of bed showing in contrast to the metal frame of the other end. If the wrong end is chosen, any further step would cause the whole trampoline to unfold and crash to the floor. Bend down and grasp the lower rail of the leg in a typical weight-lifting position: knees bent, back and arms straight, head up. Straighten the legs, lifting the whole trampoline and allowing the roller-stands to swing into a vertical position. Lower the trampoline again to rest on the wheels. If the end being held is now pushed downward, a see-saw action is set up and the legs at the other end will swing under the trampoline. As the far legs swing to their fullest extent towards the centre of the trampoline, the end being held should be lifted sharply, trapping the free-swinging leg beneath the trampoline. The lifting of this end should continue, rotating the whole trampoline about the roller-stand attachment. When the trampoline reaches the vertical position the lower legs should be lifted under the legs being held so that the weight holds the whole apparatus secure.

5. Safety Precautions After Use

There is rather an overlap between this and the last section.

Some of the points mentioned here will, of course, refer to what should be done before the actual folding of the trampoline whilst others will refer to what can only be done after the trampoline has been folded. Because of this overlap, I decided to write about the sections in this order. To keep the text as clear as possible, I will mention the factors applicable to pre-folding first and then those for after-folding.

When a session terminates, the instructor should always make a note of all deficiencies and breakages and make sure replacements are available before the trampoline is used again. The parts which usually need attention now and again are minor items which are very easy to put right: rubber cables should be rotated every so often so that the pressure is not on one point for too long. If left in its original position the rubber strands tend to break. When this happens, the corresponding cable at the other end should also be removed in order to keep the tension and throw even. If an end cable breaks, then not only should the corresponding cable at the other end be removed but also the equivalent cables on either side of the centre line. Cables should be checked regularly for wear. As soon as several strands have broken then these cables should be replaced immediately. Failure to do this could mean that a cable may snap and fly away dangerously as a performer is jumping.

With continual use, the stitching of a webbed bed is naturally inclined to break away. Any deterioration of this type must be attended to as soon as possible before pressure from the weight of a bouncer forces the weave to open wide enough to cause anxiety.

As mentioned before, the nuts holding various joints are liable to work loose. An Allan key is not always readily available during a trampoline session and, therefore, an effort should be made to tighten all these nuts at regular intervals. Loose retaining chains and difficulty with the end braces are usually the first signs that servicing is required. The large bolts holding the end braces to the frame only give visible signs of being loose when they are almost falling out. Therefore, a close check should be kept on these.

Frame pads breaking away from their attachments can be

very dangerous. When a coach stands on the frame to support a performer, or if a bouncer should land on the broken frame pads, any angular force could move the pads and the persons concerned crash to the ground. I do not suggest that new frame pads should be bought every time breakages occur but they should be tied down securely until such times as new purchases are made.

Having made all the necessary servicing checks the trampoline can now be folded. I did mention earlier about small boys being folded in the middle of the trampoline—I sincerely hope that you do not get many of these—but it is worth checking that no other articles are included at this stage. The folding satisfactorily completed, the trampoline should then be rolled away and placed in a locked storeroom. If no storeroom is available, the trampoline should be padlocked where the legs are folded across each other so that it cannot be unfolded. This will stop unauthorized people trying their skill without supervision. When the trampoline has to be left in its padlocked state where the public passes by, the side with the bed showing should be placed against a wall. Otherwise, people are inclined to rub sharp instruments along the bed, causing damage. If the trampoline has to be folded and left in the gymnasium where other activities take place, then the side with the legs showing should be placed against the wall. If a person accidentally falls against the trampoline, he will land against the bed, which is much softer than hitting the metal legs.

6. Portaging

When manually transporting a trampoline from one point to another, there are a few precautions worth remembering. First and foremost is to tie the legs together and the roller-stands securely to the folded frame; the closer to the wheels the rope is tied the firmer will be the support. Unless this is done, as soon as the wheels come into contact with any rough ground, the roller-stands will swing away and the trampoline will come crashing down. Secondly, make sure that there are sufficient helpers who are strong enough to lift the whole thing manually should the need arise. When lifting, four persons should each hold along the extension bar just above the wheels (Fig. 4). If

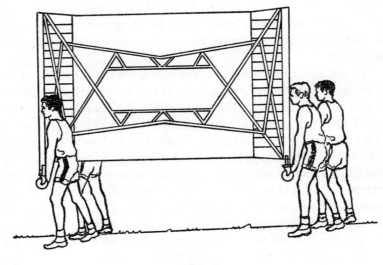

Fig. 4

further assistance is required, then these people should lift at either side (Fig. 5).

Inclement weather will mean that the bed should be removed from the frame or the whole trampoline protected by a waterproof covering. When a trampoline bed becomes wet, not only is it very uncomfortable when executing Front and Seat Drops, but it also becomes very heavy to work. Even the slightest dampness affects performance considerably. If dark clouds are imminent, take the necessary precaution; never take chances.

Damp ground, especially grass, can call for very tricky navigating, even though the trampoline is tied securely. A couple of short planks do not take up much room but they can be as useful as the caterpillar-track of a tank when manœuvring a heavy piece of apparatus. By slipping these planks under the wheels a great deal of sinking can be avoided and a passage over rough ground can also be transformed into fairly smooth going. When negotiating an incline of any gradient and surface, it is as well to

36

Fig. 5

remember to have a number of helpers at the top of the gradient pulling on a rope attached to the trampoline, as well as people pushing from behind. A slip by the people pushing, and 3 cwt. of metal could be pushing them! Not only that, it will make the weight of the trampoline less on the people who are pushing and supporting (Fig. 6).

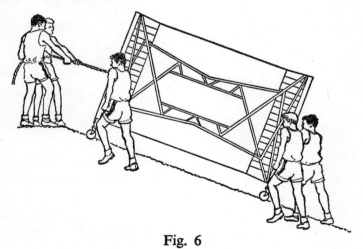

Fig. 6

37

When performing out of doors, and often this is the reason behind all the portaging, the short planks of wood which are always carried to help over damp and rough ground now serve a dual purpose. I cannot remember, in my experience, being able to set up a trampoline on a really flat surface of grass. Therefore, the short planks are placed under the legs of the trampoline in order to make the required adjustment for a level base. A person would only have to bounce once on a trampoline at an angle in order to decide never to bounce under such conditions again. To keep one's balance whilst just jumping up and down takes all one's control, but to perform any stunts is simply asking to be grounded! Please try and remember all that you have read in this chapter, because safe bouncing is enjoyable bouncing, and we want our sport to be the safest and most enjoyable there is.

2

Teaching Aids

There are many teaching aids which can be used for trampolining to enable the performer to accelerate his rate of learning or to assist a coach in putting over his methods to a pupil. Whereas it would be impossible to list all known teaching aids, I intend to mention a few of the more obvious ones which, because they are so obvious, are often forgotten—especially on coaches' examination papers! The following list is not in order of preference by any means, neither does it mean that all the aids should be used, otherwise the performer is not reaping all the benefits offered to him. A performer or a coach must be able to select particular aids appertaining to his individual needs. Those which are selected and the number required may differ from person to person; I am offering just a few. Experience will enable you to enlarge upon this list until you possess a repertoire large enough to answer all your teaching difficulties.

Coach

Whereas it is possible to teach oneself the sport of trampolining, I strongly recommend that any performer of any standard should attach himself to an experienced coach as soon as possible. There is always a right and wrong way of doing anything, but if a performer can be guided in the right direction everytime then his rate of learning must certainly be increased. In the beginning when there was no literature and there were no experienced coaches, all the pioneers of the sport had to learn through the 'trial and error' method. Although this way took longer to perfect movements, it is felt that because the person had to pass through all the incorrect positions en route, he is far more experienced as a coach to correct faulty actions than someone who has always been able to perform the perfect movement first time. As one eminent person once said, 'Experience is the best school but the fees are high!' An experienced coach can make certain that his squad progresses towards perfection along the straightest path and reaches the champion's stage in the shortest possible time. Should any from the squad divert from this straight and narrow path, then the coach can easily foretell what is the likely outcome and introduce the necessary intervening prevention. A good coach does not have to be a good performer, although this combination is very useful for demonstrating purposes. As I mentioned before, it is possible for a performer to be taught the right thing all the way through his training and never know any more than what is correct. Never having come into contact with many faults, a good performer may not necessarily be a good coach because he has not the experience of correcting movements. Here is where there is a dividing line between performer and coach: a performer is addicted to the practical side of a sport whereas the coach's forte is his vast experience through critical analysis and corrective application. In this way a coach learns through his pupils. Make use of his learning and experience if you wish to become a performer yourself; it is the safest way to success.

Books

Whether a coach or a performer, books on the subject you are pursuing are a must. No man can hope to know everything, but a collection of different ideas from different environments can combine to go a long way towards nearing the end. Having read a certain book once or twice does not mean that all the knowledge therein has been stored away in one's brain. Text books should be read and shelved for reference at some future date when a relevant problem arises. Only by reading over and over again about a particular movement, digesting it and really understanding its main points, can a person feel confident enough to put this knowledge into practice. One such man who was forced to work under these conditions because of the lack of diving coaches in his area was that very famous diver from Scotland, Peter Heatly. Peter used to read about a dive, take slow-motion film of any person already performing such a dive, and being an engineer he naturally worked out the mechanics for performing that particular movement. He would then spend a substantial amount of time studying this collection of information and when all had been thoroughly apprehended and only then, he would perform the dive from the 10 metre board exactly to his calculations. The result—British Champion for many years; Olympic Games 1948 and 1952. Peter, who was fifth in the 1948 Olympic Highboard event is an example of what can be achieved through thoroughly understanding what is required before attempting to execute a movement. This, I feel, is *the* most important factor in any activity. So learn as much as you can about your sport from any media available; a book is just one agency.

Now that we have mentioned literature I may as well continue along this vein and mention one or two other items that fall into this category.

Check-off Lists

These are most essential, especially for the pupil. The coach may be so used to teaching along certain lines and in a particular sequence that he, himself, knows of the progression a pupil is making whereas it is far more important that the pupil should know this for himself. A pupil likes to know how good he is or wants confirmation of his own beliefs, for this is perhaps the greatest means of motivation there is. Success breeds repetition and in turn correct repetition fosters further success. I have included the two types of check-off lists used by the national body as examples but any performer or coach can very easily compile his own according to his needs. The examples show separate stunts for each number but as more difficult movements are attempted then the actual build-up stages could be listed as a means of progressing to a very complex movement. The pupil then has his own check as to how near he is to success. As he sees that he only has a couple of stages to go before the full movement is achieved, then he is more likely to try harder each time in order to conquer the task. A means of motivation is very necessary throughout life and this is a good one for trampolining. (*Check-off lists are on pages* 44-45.)

Wall Charts

These are very useful when used in conjunction with the actual teaching lesson itself. The charts may be pinned to the walls or pasted on to card or hardboard and put on show at advantageous positions in close proximity to the trampoline. Whilst awaiting his turn, a pupil may be instructed to go to chart number so-and-so, read the information thereon, then study in detail the movement he is going to perform during his next turn on the trampoline. The charts may also be used in such a manner as to promote self-criticism. A pupil may be sent from the trampoline to study a certain chart in order to determine for himself why he was not successful at his last attempt at the stunt, wherefrom he returns to the coach to discuss the deductions of his findings. Here again, a coach may make up his own collection of charts and write below each figural performer the important points which may be insisted upon during teaching and coaching periods. To have a visual support to oral instructions can only prove beneficial. Wall charts may even brighten up the room and provide the correct atmosphere and attitude for your class.

Films

At this point I am going to include films and a few other teaching aids which together with wall charts make up our collection of visual aids. The most important factor which movie film has over all other types of visual aid is that it can be stopped at any time by using an analysing projector. This is most useful when discussing aerial body positions or techniques. The performer may be seen in slow-motion which is an ideal medium for studying any sequence of movements and, by using loops, certain movements can be seen over and over again to saturation point so that the brain is completely subjected to autosuggestion. When the time comes for the performer to execute a movement the mind is properly prepared to supply the body with the necessary information. The body, of course, must have followed through all the correct lead-up stages in readiness for this particular movement and only when both the mind and the body are completely ready should a performer be asked to execute the final stage. I regard movie film as one of the most important contributory factors to success in aerial activity if used properly.

Good Performer

In just about every squad there is at least one good performer who can be used for demonstration purposes if the coach is not a presentable performer himself. The reasons for a demonstration of all teaching and coaching methods are the same as for those mentioned earlier:

1. To support the coach's statement.
2. To thrust home what is required.
3. To allow self-analysis by the audience.
4. To prove that it is humanly possible.

This last factor bears more importance than one may, at first, realize. The top performers in this sport of trampolining have reached the end of the line of reality and now stand on the threshold of supererogation. Movements such as triple somersaults—quadruple twisting somersaults—and double somersaults with twists, which it may be possible to see under circumstances other than trampolining, have all been mastered already! The sport which is still in its infancy seems to have no ceiling. Like the track races in athletics, where records are continually being broken, there must be a human limit sometime, but when? The four-minute mile was just a dream, until a human being by the name of Roger Bannister broke this barrier. Since the psychological barrier had been overcome by one man, others followed suit and in London in 1965, eight competitors in

43

Personal Check-off List

Name.. Group...

1. Bouncing and checking ....
2. Tuck bouncing ....
3. Straddle bouncing ....
4. Seat Drop ....
5. Hands and Knees Drop ....
6. Knee Drop..
7. Front Drop from Hands and Knees Drop ....
8. Front Drop from standing ....
9. Back Drop ....
10. All the above bounces performing each 5 times consecutively ....
11. Knee to seat ....
12. Seat to Front Drop ....
13. Front to Seat Drop ....
14. Back Drop to Front Drop ....
15. Front Drop to Back Drop ....
16. Combination of 4 or more bounces ....
17. $\frac{1}{2}$-twist to Front Drop ....
18. $\frac{1}{2}$-twist to Back Drop ....
19. $\frac{1}{2}$-turntable ....
20. Knee bounce $\frac{1}{2}$-twist to seat ....
21. Seat $\frac{1}{2}$-twist to seat (Swivel Hips) ....
22. Seat bounce full-twist to seat ....
23. Back Drop forward half-twist to back (Cradle) ....
24. Back Drop full-twist to back (Cat-twist)..............................
25. Knee bounce roll forward (Bent Dive) ....
26. Knee bounce turnover to seat ....
27. Standing bent dive over to back then feet ....
28. Standing bent dive over to seat ....
29. Knee bounce forward somersault to feet ....
30. Standing forward somersault to feet ....
31. Two or more forward bounce rolls ....
32. Back Pull-over to hands and knees ....
33. Bent knee seat bounce into a back-over to feet ....
34. Back somersault with assistance ....
35. Back somersault unaided feet to feet ....
36. Back somersault to hands and knees ....
37. Routine of 6 different bounces ....
38. Routine of 8 different bounces ....
39. Knee bounce handstand, $\frac{1}{2}$-twist to knees ....
40. Knee bounce Barani to knees ....
41. Knee bounce Barani to feet ....
42. Barani feet to feet ....
43. Layout Back somersault ....
44. Layout three-quarter Back to Front Drop ....
45. Front Drop, forward turnover to Back Drop ....

44

Advanced Personal Check-off List

Name..   Group....................

1. Back Drop forward ½-twist to Back Drop (Cradle) ....
2. Seat Drop full-twist to Seat Drop.......................................
3. Seat Drop vertical 1½-twist to Seat Drop.................................
4. Back Drop full-twist to Back Drop (Cat-twist) ....
5. Back Drop full-twist to feet ....
6. Back Drop 1½-twist to feet ....
7. Back Drop forward 1½-twist to Back Drop (Corkscrew) ....
8. Back Drop forward turnover to Seat Drop.................................
9. Back Drop forward somersault to feet (Ball out) ....
10. Back Drop, back somersault ....
11. Back Drop, ½ twisting back to feet (Baby Fliffus) ....
12. Three Cradles or Cat-twists in swing time ....
13. Repeat (12 above) twisting in opposite direction ....
14. Vertical jump with full-twist to Back Drop.............................
15. Front Drop, full turntable ....
16. Front Drop, 1½ turntable ....
17. Front Drop, vertical rise with ½-twist and forward turnover to back.....
18. Back Drop, inverted vertical arch, three times in swing ....
19. Front Drop, forward turnover to Seat Drop ....
20. Front Drop, forward somersault (Front Cody) ....
21. Front Drop, Barani to feet...
22. Knee bounce front somersault to feet ....
23. Knee bounce 1½ front somersault to Front Drop ....
24. Knee bounce, Barani to feet ....
25. Repeat twisting in opposite direction ....
26. Knee bounce full twisting forward turnover to Back Drop ....
27. Forward somersault unaided without travel ....
28. Forward somersault piked position ....
29. Forward turnover in pike with full-twist to seat.......................
30. Forward somersault with full-twist to feet ....
31. Forward somersault with 1½-twist.......................................
32. Backward somersault without aid or travel..............................
33. Backward somersault into forward turnover to seat ....
34. Backward somersault into forward somersault without travel.............
35. Backward somersault into Barani ....
36. Three backward somersaults in swing without travel ....
37. Three forward somersaults in swing without travel ....
38. Barani unaided and without travel ....
39. Barani into forward turnover to seat ....
40. Barani into forward somersault without travel ....
41. Side somersault (Barrel Roll)..
42. Layout back somersault to feet ....
43. Layout back somersault with ½-twist ....
44. Layout back somersault with full-twist ....
45. Back somersault with 1½ twist ....
46. Back somersault with double twist ....
47. ½ back somersault to Front Drop (Lazy Back) ....
48. Lazy Back with ½-twist to Seat Drop....................................
49. Three Baranis in swing without travel ....
50. A swing time routine of 6 different bounces ....
51. A swing time routine of 8 different bounces ....
52. Any 10 bounce swing time routine ....
53. Back Drop Kaboom to Front Drop ....
54. Back Drop to Kaboom to feet ....
55. Back Drop Kaboom to seat ....
56. Back Drop Kaboom to Back Drop ....
57. Double back or front somersault with support in overhead rig...........
58. Double back or front somersault without aid............................
59. Overturned Barani to Back Drop ....
60. Back or front, half or full, late or early Fliffus ....

45

the same race crashed through the tape in under four minutes! Mount Everest stood unconquered for thousands of years, an impossible climb! But in 1953 a team of men under the leadership of John Hunt overcame this mental obstruction and now Everest has become a popular climb with fourteen successful parties in one year. So, to prove that something is humanly possible is very important, especially when stepping out into the field of the unknown as we are in trampolining. Men must now invent their own movements, unknown in other spheres, and when they do others will follow.

Adjustable Doll

This is useful for showing the correct positions required when no suitable performer is available, and can be made from various substances and in different shapes ranging from metal to rubber and from a flat silhouette to a fully proportioned figure. The nursery rubber doll used to be popular in the beginning but the general feeling today is towards a flat silhouette since better body positions may be achieved. The doll's greatest attribute is its use in the explanation of the mechanics involved in trampolining. Any body position can be formed and its position in the air in relation to the movement required is very easily obtained. This method is far easier and far more successful than trying to contort one's own body into gravity-defying situations and never truly attaining the correct one. To make a silhouette model all that is required is a drawing of a man standing upright, toes pointed and arms stretched straight forward in front of himself. Trace each part of the doll on to the material to be used for the finished product. There should be one head, one body and at least one each of the following: upper arm (shoulder to elbow); lower arm (elbow to wrist); hands; upper leg (hip to knee); lower leg (knee to ankle); foot. Pin all these parts together in their conventional order at the points where maximum mobility usually occurs. A dab of paint and the doll and its master are ready for action.

TEACHING AIDS

Blackboard and Chalk

Obviously, this must be the oldest type of visual aid (perhaps in a different form) that there is. Scratchings and drawings have retold history in all parts of the world. A great deal of information can be derived from, or made clear through, a few marks placed in just the right position and combined with the all-important verbal explanation. The advantages of this medium are that it is quick; it is portable; the diagrams may be adjusted at any time during conversations; new subjects can be discussed at a moment's notice; and it is on the spot available for reference throughout any session. Normally, films and wall charts are compiled commercially and a coach has to take what is offered to him, but by using the blackboard and chalk a coach is able to produce exactly what he wants, when he wants and how he wants it.

Spotters

These really do come under the heading of teaching aids. When learning, whether it be a basic bounce or the most complicated movement on record, every bouncer likes to have the satisfaction of knowing that someone is there to save him should things go wrong and also to watch him perform his particular stunt. To feel confident that an all-out effort can be put into a movement without having to worry too much about the landing is half-way to success. All too often a performer does not master a movement because there has not been sufficient confidence on take-off. Therefore, more spotters, more confidence—and more confidence, more success. Secondly, there must be a purpose for doing anything. In a large number of cases the aim is recognition—what is the use of doing something if nobody knows you have done it! To attempt a new movement when the eyes of all the spotters are upon you gives one the incentive to succeed. If spotters can induce even the slightest modicum of success then they certainly are a teaching aid.

47

Gymnastic Belt

This is usually a broad band of webbing approximately 4 in. wide with buckles at the front and rear. These buckles enable the belt to be adjusted to fit most sizes of waist and also to fasten the belt securely. At each side there should be a swivel clip to enable the wearer to rotate about a lateral axis freely. To these clips should be fastened a length of rope, preferably nylon, so that assistants may support the performer safely. By standing on the frame of the trampoline, or on a vaulting-box beside and at the same height as the frame, one or two assistants may sustain the weight of the performer during a somersaulting movement. Where two assistants are used, naturally one will stand on each side of the trampoline. Besides giving support, a belt gives confidence to the performer. This will enable him to make an attempt at a movement which, perhaps, he would never try without the aid of the belt. Having received the 'feel' of the full movement, the performer may then be ready to undertake the same without the superfluous aid.

Towel

A towel will assist in all the ways in which a gymnastic belt will assist but with a few subtle differences. A towel is softer on the performer's body and will not cut into his skin. When an assistant has been supporting a number of bouncers during a session he is apt to perspire. This perspiration on his hands makes it difficult for the assistant to grasp the nylon rope securely. Towelling will soak up any moisture on the hands thereby making its use more efficient. It is very easy and quick to wrap a towel around a person's waist as there are no buckles and straps to fasten. Also there is no time lag between performing with support and performing without. Lastly, a belt may not always be available whereas a towel is naturally an important item of a trampolinist's kit and, therefore, always to hand.

16. Floor models may be erected anywhere, whether it be indoors or out.

17. (*Right*) Gary Erwin, 1965 World Champion, performing a back somersault, piked.

18. Valerie Hadley of the Bexley Gym Club showing the hip lift when performing a Backdrop.

19. Valerie Hadley performing a half twist to frontdrop.

20. A professional act using another method of assisting whilst performing a Barani.

21. Gary Erwin, 1965 World Amateur Champion and 1967 World Professional Champion, performing a Barani.

Twisting Belt

This is similar to the gymnastic belt but has an additional item of two concentric rings, one rotating inside the other. The conflicting surfaces of the rings are of either extremely smooth plastic or else separated by ball-bearings to reduce friction. By wearing this type of belt a performer may execute movements where he needs to rotate about two different axes at the same time. This is an extremely useful piece of equipment when learning fliffus movements; should the performer fail to execute the full movement safely he can be held off the bed by the person manipulating the supporting ropes. The belt is best used in conjunction with an overhead pulley system, attached either to the ceiling or a spotting rig.

Spotting Rig

This is a metal frame with built-in pulleys which is manufactured specially to support a performer by means of ropes and a belt (Fig. 7). The frame is in five separate pieces which makes for easy carriage. Each piece slots tightly into the other and is then secured by an Allan nut. Part A is the top and incorporates the pulleys, double at one end (G) and single at the other (H). The lower section (C), rests on the floor on two wheels (F), which means that when rigged, a trampoline may be moved from one point to another without dismantling. At point (C) there is a protrusion which engages into the sleeve used for the roller stand attachment. (E) is a locking arm which is bolted to the frame of the trampoline in order to hold the rig steady. One arm is secured to one side of the upright whilst the arm on the other side of the trampoline is bolted on the opposite side. The (B) section is purely an extension of (C) in order to give the performer room to execute intricate movements. The whole rig is assembled on the floor and the ropes properly passed through the pulleys before the whole contraption is finally secured to the trampoline. The spotting rig is ideal where all bouncing is performed out of doors or where the trampoline has to be moved

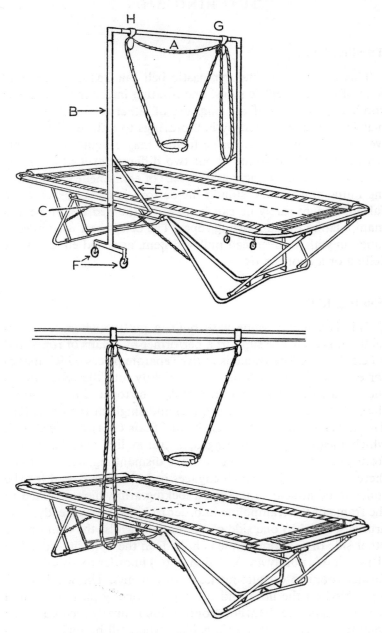

Fig. 7

around the gymnasium to different positions to allow for other activities to take place. If all the trampolining in your club is to be indoors and in one set place then it may be more beneficial for you to have your spotting rig as a permanent structure bolted direct to the ceiling. Select a stout beam or metal joist and bolt on the single and double pulleys at the most advantageous position beneath which the trampoline can be permanently situated.

In order to make sure that the distance between the pulleys and the necessary 45° angles are correct, the simple formula of W=2H—13 is used. In this case W stands for width and the H for height. Therefore, supposing that the height of the gymnasium was 24 ft., W=2 × 24—13.

W=48—13.

W=35 ft.

When using an overhead rig, the following points should be remembered:

(a) If there is not a correct angle of 45° then the system will not be able to function properly, since the attachment between the ropes and the performer consists of two swivel-hooks, one on either side. If the angle is incorrect the swivels and the performer will be rotating about different axes.

(b) Always use nylon rope since this is more reliable; and make certain that the cut ends are sealed in a flame. Holding a lighted match to the ends is quite satisfactory.

(c) Never let the rope become too tangled before releasing the kinks.

(d) The performer should wear a long-sleeved jumper, or similar, as a means of protection against rope burns. Some supporters handling the ropes prefer to protect their hands by wearing old leather gloves.

(e) When not in use, make sure that the belt is pulled high into the girders or unclipped and the side ropes secured to the side supports or frame.

(f) The performer must always bounce in the centre of the bed and beneath the centre of the two overhead pulleys, otherwise a definite pendulum swinging action will take place.

Not only will it be very difficult to execute the movement correctly but the supporter will also find it almost impossible to give any assistance to the uncontrolled flyer.

(g) The bouncer must always keep his arms in front of the ropes and his legs together when performing a movement or he may become entangled in the ropes.

(h) The supporter must try to ensure that there is no slackness in the ropes to cause the performer's arms to become entangled as this would mean a very uncomfortable jerk on his body should a save have to be made suddenly.

Diving Board

This piece of apparatus comes into its own when the more complicated movements are being learned: the multiple somersaults, the multiple twisting movements and the combinations of these two. The spotting rigs may be all right for some things but there comes a time when there is no room for an outside encumbrance. This is the occasion when the body is called upon to give all its energies towards the closest tucks, the fastest spins and the snappiest movements. The fliffus and triffus are the movements where performing from a diving board can be most helpful. The diving boards of today are being manufactured with a recoil which is very similar to that of a trampoline. Therefore, a trampolinist will very soon get the 'feel' of the board. The only adjustment that must be made is that for travelling away from the board, but whereas a diver aims at keeping this down to a minimum, the trampolinist needs only to worry about clearing the board. The diver's main interest is what he can do from the time he leaves the board until the time he enters the water. Getting a great deal of height from the board is not necessary since a 3-metre springboard is already nearly 10 ft. from the water. As for the entry into the water, the only time this could be painful is if the performer landed flat, and this could be diminished if he wore a light jumper. The dangers of awkward landings or throwing off the trampoline are eliminated. I feel that at the moment this method is not used enough in this country because trampolinists feel that they have to bounce the

board absolutely correctly before they dare to try out trampolining movements. In America trampolinists and divers work
out regularly from each other's apparatus; I hope that it will not
be too long before these two sports in Britain work together in
closer harmony and each accepts what the other has to offer in
mutual benefit.

3

Types of Equipment—Advantages and Disadvantages

Frames

There are three basic types of frame on the market.
1. The rigid type which cannot be folded or taken to pieces.
2. The type which has been constructed so that the legs may be dismantled and the frame itself can pull apart.
3. The folding model which normally folds into three sections. The legs also fold and the whole framework can be rotated to the vertical position on roller-stands for easy transporting and storage.

RIGID TYPE

Advantages. None.
Disadvantages. Cumbersome to move around; storage problems; transporting difficulties.

DISMANTLING TYPE

Advantages. It can be transported and stored easily.
Disadvantages. The bed and the suspension system have to be removed each time after use. Takes time to prepare for use. Continual dismantling with metal clashing against metal and concrete will, in time, cause damage.

FOLDING TYPE

Advantages. Ease of transportation and storage; tension on the suspension system and bed released simply by folding. Quick, easy action for immediate use. Great time-saving factor in preparation and termination of bouncing sessions.

Disadvantages. In each section there are models of varying heights from the ground. It must be remembered, however, that these have advantages and disadvantages according to use. The lower models are ideal for children since they do not have so far to climb when mounting and dismounting, whereas an adult using a small model could touch the ground when performing. It is, therefore, purely a matter of use.

Beds

Again, there are many different types of bed ranging from the single thickness solid nylon sheet to the string bed. The single thickness solid nylon sheet is the cheapest type available and is fairly light to work but, as with all solid beds, the performer is more inclined to slip than with the web bed as the make-up of the webbing gives more traction to the surface. The double thickness solid bed naturally increases the price and is heavier for the performer to use, but it should last longer. There is also an opportunity to invert the bed so that a clean surface can be presented when the other has become dirty. Another advantage that a solid nylon bed has over the web bed is that it is easier to wash.

The first of the web beds was made of $1\frac{3}{4}$-in. broad nylon strands and its introduction caused great interest. The difference in performance between these two surfaces seemed to be so vast that everyone wanted to bounce on this new system, and this interest and demand caused a great development in web beds. Later, a 1-in. web bed came upon the scene and its lightness and lively performance immediately showed its advantage over the heavier $1\frac{3}{4}$-in. webbing—$\frac{5}{8}$-in., $\frac{1}{2}$-in. and string beds appeared on the market in quick succession. From the choice of beds now offered it seems that the ½-in. web is the most popular. The disadvantages of the string bed are that it is so light that a heavy performer can depress the bed to the ground, which is very dangerous. Also, the mesh is so fine that the performer finds it very difficult to focus on the bed when executing the more advanced movements.

Now that we know of the different types of beds available let us look more closely into the advantages and disadvantages of solid and web beds.

ADVANTAGES

Solid Beds

Cheaper. Very important when working to a budget.

Safer for beginners, since a wide area of the bed is depressed when a performer lands on it as opposed to the two individual indentations made by the feet on a web bed. The point to remember, however, is that the rate of progress is so rapid with trampolining that a newcomer to the sport is not a beginner for long.

Cleaning the bed by washing with a detergent is made easier because of the flat, smooth surface.

Web Beds

Wide choice of different types.

Livelier recoil, because the webbing allows the air to flow through the holes when the bed is being worked. This permits more difficult stunts to be executed.

Lighter in weight and, therefore, coupled with the livelier recoil this makes bouncing less exhausting.

More satisfying because of the ease with which stunts can be performed. Also a whole new field of more advanced movements is within the reach of the performers, hence more motivation, incentive and opportunity to succeed.

Grip. The overlapping of the webbing strands and the stitching holding them in place give greater traction than with the solid bed.

DISADVANTAGES

Solid Beds

Slippery. The smooth surface is inclined to make the performer slip on difficult landings.

Air resistance. The large area of the solid sheet displaces a great deal of air when depressed. The air is forced out to the sides creating a vacuum when the bed begins its recoil. Because of this, the bed is *heavy to work and the recoil is slow and weak*.

Burns. The smooth nylon surface can cause slight burns especially on elbows and knees when bad landings are performed. For this reason the wearing of long-sleeved garments and gymnastic trousers or track-suits is recommended.

Web Beds

Price. More expensive than solid beds, and the price increases with the finer web.

More control is required since the feet make two independent indentations. This means that the slightest increase in weight on one foot will throw the performer to the side. I hasten to add that experienced performers can very quickly adjust their actions to counteract this.

Washing. Because of the number of holes in the bed cleaning becomes more difficult.

Stitching. Each strand of webbing has two or sometimes three rows of stitching along its length. Where these strands overlap there is a pulling-apart action in different directions when someone is bouncing. In time, this naturally causes the stitching to wear and break. The bed then has to be returned to the manufacturer to be re-stitched.

The holes can cause the breaking of finger and toe-nails should the performer fail to keep them at a reasonable length or bounce without footwear. But sometimes, however, the holes can be used to an advantage, especially when performing a turn-table where the finger-tips can lodge in the holes for a really efficient grip.

57

Grazes. Because of the better grip which a web bed gives it is obvious that this extra traction can only come from a rougher surface. This means that badly performed landings could result in grazing the skin.

ADVANTAGES

Springs

Price. Approximately one-third of the price of cables.

Fast recoil. Because of their strength, there is an extremely good force of recoil when they are reasonably new. As the years pass some of this strength is lost.

Cables

Range of choice. There are various types starting with the single cable with a hook on each end; these are manufactured for cheapness but have no life-span. There are those which have the ends clipped together or pass through a buckle. This type has two freely running hooks or rings on each cable so that the cables may be *adjustable* for length and also for wear and tear. There is also the endless rubber cable which permits it to be rotated and moved through the ring-hooks so that positions of stress and strain may be fully variable. Lastly there is the double thickness cable with fixed hooks at either end. With the use of *extension hooks* an infinite range of adjustment in length is possible from $\frac{1}{2}$-in. onwards in units of $\frac{1}{2}$-in.

Noiseless. When being worked; an important factor where other activities are taking place at the same time or during competition.

Softer. Should a performer move too close to the suspension system, the softness of the rubber cable does not injure the person.

Recoil. The rubber suspension system produces a smoother, softer action which extends the cables further and, therefore, results in a higher recoil.

Interchangeability. Cables may be fitted and changed very quickly and simply. No special tool is required as is the case with springs.

58

Flexibility. Should a performer land directly upon the cables they will return to their natural state and the elasticity will not rupture.

DISADVANTAGES

Springs

Noisy. Metal continually playing against metal. Liable to *rust.*

Fixing. A special tool in the shape of a hook has to be used so that when being pulled into position the tension is over the whole range rather than just one section, which could cause the spring to rupture.

Flexibility. Any sudden strain directly on a section of a spring can cause a rupture in its elasticity.

Harder. Should a performer accidentally land on a metal spring it is liable to injure this person in some way. Because of the manner in which a spring is constructed it is possible for the skin to be *pinched* when contact is made during its recoil.

The *attachment hooks* are of a narrower gauge and, therefore, are sharper and may cause damage to a performer.

Cables

Cost. They are almost three times more expensive than springs. Because the make-up of rubber is inconsistent the *throw* is uneven.

ADVANTAGES

Pit Models

The main purpose and advantage of a pit model is that it enables a trampoline to be used indoors when normally the *ceiling height* would prohibit this activity. By covering the pit with floor boards there is no wastage of *space* when storing.

Floor Models

Transportable. A floor model may be erected anywhere, whether it be indoors or out.

Most suitable for *display work* for this reason.

Much *safer*. Should a performer be falling on to, or past, the frame, he can grasp the framework allowing his body to swing to the ground feet first. His head is then kept clear of major injury.

Spotters are technically in a more effective position since they can get beneath the weight of a falling performer.

The problem of *air cushioning* and overcoming the *vacuum* created whilst bouncing was mentioned under the section relating to the comparison of types of beds. It again enters into this section since by far the vast majority of air that is displaced escapes out around the sides of the trampoline.

DISADVANTAGES

Pit Models

Not transportable.

Dust collecting in the pit is very awkward to remove. When bouncing, a mild dust storm is produced making it very uncomfortable for anyone executing Front Drops. With the four sides of the trampoline enclosed, the *air which is displaced* can only infiltrate through the suspension system and through the webbing, if a web bed is used. This is an impediment which makes bouncing very *hard work* and the recoil very *slow*.

Spotters find it difficult to catch effectively because at the crucial moment they are standing beside the performer rather than beneath him.

Psychologically the performer is at a disadvantage, especially having bounced on a floor model, because he has a feeling of insufficient height above the heads of the spotters. When contemplating an advanced movement this psychological effect may cause a performer to 'chicken-out' for no real reason.

4

The Basic Mechanics Involved in Trampolining

In order to analyse movement correctly it is most important that the mechanics creating the movement are understood. Too many people believe that the science of movement is so involved and complex that they brush it aside and hope to rely upon common sense and experience only. Perhaps the science of mechanics is very complex when taken to its extremity but this only makes it all the more intriguing and interesting. The human senses have been known to play many strange tricks on us from time to time. By relying upon these alone we may find that we imagine and believe that a certain action is producing a certain movement, when scientifically this can be proved impossible. By gaining even the slightest knowledge of mechanics we have a third dimension, which has been proved infallible throughout the centuries, upon which to base our reasoning.

One point which I feel should be mentioned here is that the mechanics applied to aerial skills are not always constant. There are a number of dominant factors which can differ in individuals as well as places. Among these are the weight and size of a person compared with his muscular strength and the differences between the total lengths over which muscles have to operate— that is, the differences in the origins and insertions of the muscles and the moving angles of muscle attachments as limbs move. Then there are all the changing elements of the atmosphere; differing amounts of air resistance, etc. Although these factors may not make all that amount of difference to the per-

61

formance, they are worth remembering when a certain movement does not produce the exact result expected. I mention them because the mechanics in sport are based on scientific reasoning where the governing factors are constant. Therefore, there is a slight variation between the two.

I intend here to cover the very basics of the mechanics which are involved in trampolining. I shall keep the wording very simple in order to encourage people of all ages to take an interest in this subject and understand what is involved. If you find that it also begins to interest you, I sincerely hope that you will continue to pursue its channels beyond the realms of this chapter.

I am going to discuss the basic mechanical laws only and give examples of their application. They are Newton's Laws of Motion.

Law 1. 'A mass will remain at rest or at a constant linear speed until other forces are impressed upon it.' This means that all objects and persons would remain perfectly still indefinitely if *something* did not make them move. A performer standing on the trampoline must depress the bed before he can be thrown into the air. Muscular energy has to be directed through the legs to depress the bed and then an equivalent recoil from the bed will project the performer into the air.

Law 2. 'The impressed forces alter the direction of the mass in units per force equal to the resultant product of the forces.' The second law states that having once initiated any momentum, this speed will continue in a straight line until other forces slow it down, stop it, reverse it or change its direction. The natural elements continually affect the progress of a mass. The wind, or even just the atmosphere, is sufficient to cause this change. Friction and gravity have an even greater control over a moving mass and all of these must be taken into consideration when analysing certain movements.

Law 3. 'For every action there is an equal and opposite reaction.' This means that for every displacement of weight around the centre of gravity of a mass, an equivalent adjustment in weight must take place in a corresponding area in order to keep the centre of gravity constant. Without this adjustment the mass will become unbalanced. An example of this would be someone practising a friction skill such as ski-ing or skating, where any loss of balance is followed by arms swinging and hips swinging in order to readjust the body weight around the centre of gravity.

Now let us review these laws and see how they apply to trampolining. 'A mass will remain at rest or at a constant linear speed until other forces are impressed upon it.' This is also known as the law of inertia, since it asserts that no body can alter its state of rest or motion without outside influence; in other words, every body has inertia. Imagine a football in a state of rest in the middle of a field. This football would continue to remain stationary until someone propelled it forward, we will say by kicking it. Having been set in motion this ball would roll on at a constant speed until some external force acted upon it. Thinking of the times when we, ourselves, play ball games it is quite easy to see what is likely to act upon the ball. There is the friction incurred through rolling along the ground under the influence of gravity and the thicker the grass, or wetter the mud, the more rapidly the ball will slow down its rate of progress. Sky a ball on a windy day and the same result of another force can be seen. Kick the ball straight into the arms of the goalkeeper and it no longer continues at its constant linear speed. All these are examples of other forces being impressed on the ball which alter its original state. As a performer, one could remain 'at rest' on the bed and allow the spotters, as 'another force', to depress the bed and kip the performer into the air—or, as one usually does, exert muscular energy through one's legs to push the bed away so that the recoil will set the body in motion. Another method whereby it is possible to get an equal and opposite recoil from the bed is by swinging the arms upwards vigorously. If this action was to be performed consecutively, and the timing of each upward swing was to coincide with the bed being depressed to its fullest each time, then there would be an increase in the recoil from the bed. Try this test for yourself whilst kneeling on the bed. Having left the bed the body should continue to rise until some external force acts upon it. Such forces could include the roof, if it was exceptionally low, gravity and air resistance. Because these elements are with us constantly, it is impossible for a trampolinist, after one bounce, to fly through the clouds to eternity. It must be remembered, however, that we are battling against these forces all the time in order to gain more height throughout a routine.

The 'impressed forces which alter the direction of a mass, in units per force, equal to the resultant product of these forces' may best be illustrated by referring to our football once again. Imagine a beautiful pass has been made and the ball is rolling forward at a force of 10 units. Let us also imagine for a moment that there were no factors to slow down this ball so that its rate of progress was constant. Another player, to whom the pass was made, wishes to redirect the ball to a third player standing 45° in front of him. The player deflecting the ball could then either strike the ball at 90° with an equal force of 10 units so that the resultant product of these forces was half forward and sideways, therefore, obtaining the required 45°, or the second player could strike the ball with a stronger force but with a correspondingly more acute angle towards the third player. When applied to trampolining perhaps, for our purpose, the Swivel Hips movement is the best example. A performer dropping on to the trampoline bed in the sitting position from a height will receive an upward thrust from the suspension system. So long as he remains perfectly balanced he will be projected into the air and return to the same spot on the bed still in his Seat Drop. If, as the body was rising, however, the hands were to push against the bed at one end of this rising body then another force would have been brought into action. The rise of the body would then be in the direction of the resultant product of these two forces, i.e. upward and with forward rotation. Should one of the hands, during the action of pushing, apply more force than the other then a third force would add its momentum to that of the others. The effect would then be upward thrust, forward rotation and lateral rotation, which together in the correct proportions result in the Swivel Hips. This is only one method of performing a Swivel Hips.

The third law tells us that 'for every action there is an equal and opposite reaction.' Let us look at the football again. The harder a ball is thrown to the ground, the higher will be its rebound. If it is only dropped from a low height then the reaction

22. Beverley Averyt, U.S.A., performing her 'Out Bounce' during the competition G.B. v. U.S.A., 1965.

23. Gary Erwin performing a back somersault with triple twist.

24. Pat Winkle, British Trampoline Champion in 1963, instructing members of the Crystal Palace football team at Crystal Palace National Recreation Centre, 1965.

25. (*Right*) Lynn Davies, performing the winning Long Jump of 26 ft. 5½ in. during the Tokyo Olympics, 1964.

26. (*Below*) Joe Senior at the Trampoline Conference in London demonstrating the use of this equipment by a totally blind boy.

will be a low bounce. A similar reaction takes place when bouncing. The greater the height from which a performer drops on to the bed, the more he will depress the bed by extending the suspension system. In contrast, the cables would have to move through a greater range in order to return to their normal state, thereby catapulting the performer higher into the air. Another example of this third law is very prominent during the execution of a Piked Straddle Jump. As the legs are raised upward there is an equal displacement of body mass by the arms and upper half of the trunk in moving downward. At the same time as the legs and trunk move forward, the hips counter-balance this movement by moving backward. In order to test the validity of this statement, stand in the middle of a room and bend down to touch your toes with straight legs—easy! Now stand with your back flat against a wall and your heels pressed hard against the skirting board; try to touch your toes again. You will find that this time the wall does not allow room for your hips to move backward as your body moves forward, with the result that you fall over.

Knowledge of the different classes of lever is also most important to anyone who wishes to analyse movement and apply his experience to all the bouncers seeking his advice. Very conveniently, these different types of lever fall into three classes similar to Newton's Laws of Motion.

Class 1 is where the fulcrum (F) is situated somewhere along the length of the bar between the weight (W) to be raised and the

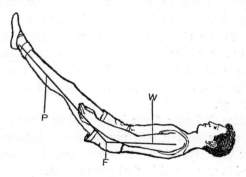

Fig. 8

power (P) to do the raising. Its application to trampolining can be illustrated easily when performing a Back Drop to Front Drop movement (Fig. 8). The longer the lever, the stronger the force it applies and in trampolining this means the easier the movement.

Class 2 is when the weight is positioned somewhere along the length of the bar and the power and the fulcrum are on either side of the weight and towards the end of the bar. In trampolining the Seat Drop is a good example (Fig. 9).

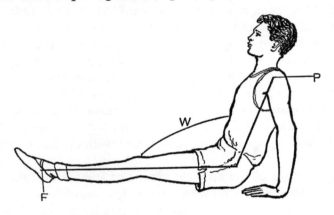

Fig. 9

Class 3 is where the power is situated somewhere along the bar between the weight and the fulcrum. The Back Pull-over where the hands are used to push against the bed may be used as the simplest illustration of this type of lever (Fig. 10).

Apart from the above principal explanations of mechanics there are a number of terms which will be used from time to time in the chapters which follow. I will list them here in order to help the reader understand what is meant by their application when the time comes.

Acceleration. When a force is applied to a mass in the direction of its movement it will progressively increase its rate of progress or velocity. This increase in speed is known as acceleration and is measured in feet per second.

Centre of Gravity (applied to take-off). When the centre of gravity falls within the base of the body then it is said to be in a state of equilibrium, or stable. If the centre of gravity is in front of the base on take-off, a travelling somersault will be produced. The travelling follows the direction of the position of the centre of gravity, when force is applied to the base of the body.

Centrifugal Force. A term employed to denote the force with which a body moving round a centre tends to fly away from that centre. A simple example is that of a small weight rapidly rotated in a circle at the end of a string held in the hand. The string being in a state of tension, is thus exerting a force on the weight, tending to draw it towards the hand. The weight exercises an equal and opposite force outwards. If the string was to be cut suddenly, or the holder was to release his grip, the weight would fly off at a tangent in the direction in which it was moving at the moment of release.

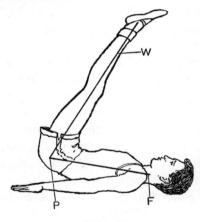

Fig. 10

Couple. A pair of equal forces acting in parallel and opposite directions so as to impart a circular movement. Working on the same principle as is explained for the *Moment of Force.* There will be more effect on the body from a long lever than from a shorter lever of the same weight, when both are moved through the same number of degrees and with the same amount of angular velocity. When rotating about an axis, the greater the radius of gyration the slower will be the angular velocity. In twisting movements about the longitudinal axis, the closer the arms are brought towards this axis the faster will be the twist. In somersaulting, the centre of gravity becomes the axis about which the body will spin. Once again, the closer that the mass of the body can get to this point the faster will be the rotation. With rotations, or angular motion, there will always be a centrifugal force, which is an antagonistic factor with which we must contend.

Force. That which causes, stops, or alters motion in a body. This force is measured in pounds and the method used to determine its weight is the amount of gravitational force used to move the mass at 45° at sea level. As the weight depends on the quantity of its mass and its positions near to the centre of the earth, it will vary from place to place.

Force of Gravity—or gravitational attraction—is imposed upon all freely falling bodies at the rate of 32 ft. per second. This velocity is nearly constant and may be taken as such for our purposes.

Inertia. That property of a body by which it persists in an existing state of rest or of uniform motion in a straight line unless an external force changes that state. The mass of a body resists being set in motion but when it is set in motion, either linear or angular, it continues this velocity until stopped by some other force. The heavier the mass, the more force will be necessary to set it in motion and, conversely, the more force will be required to bring the mass to a stop.

Linear and Angular Motion. A force applied to a mass will cause the mass to travel with linear or angular motion or both. If there is angular motion the mass will rotate about a given centre. If one end of the mass is fixed then this will be the point around which the mass will rotate. In the case of the body, the rotation will be about the nearest joint if the end is secured to a fixed support. If the body is revolving in space then the centre of rotation will be the centre of gravity of that body.

Moment of Force. This is the force applied to the end of a lever or radius of gyration to produce a rotary action. It is calculated by measuring the amount of *force* x, *the perpendicular distance from the axis used.* We call this perpendicular the 'moment arm'.

68

In everyday language it proves that a short lever requires less force than a longer lever to move it through the same number of degrees.

Momentum. The quantity of motion in a body. This is equal to *the mass* × *the velocity at which it is travelling*. When momentum is transferred from one part of the body to the whole body, *the mass* × *the velocity of the part* must equal *the mass* × *the velocity of the whole*. Where the mass is of a light weight, its product must be made up by a high degree of velocity.

Torque. The movement of a system of force causing rotation. This term is applied to a force which is transmitted through an axis. One end of the axis is held in a fixed position. When the fixed position is released the whole body will rotate around this axis.

Velocity. The distance the body travels through a unit of time in feet per second, miles per hour, etc.

Principles of Twisting. Although twisting movements will be explained in a later chapter, some insight into the principles involved in creating twists is required in order fully to understand their application. Firstly, let us take a twisting jump. If the performer were to jump straight into the air in the straight position and then throw an arm across the body whilst still in this straight position, there would be an equal and opposite reaction and the body would turn in the other direction. Because the weight of a person's arm is slight compared with the weight of his body, the amount of reactional twist is small. The arm would have to be thrown across the body many times before a half-twist jump could be executed using this technique. However, as soon as the arm is brought away from the body the reaction occurs again and the body returns to its original position. If we look back to the section on levers, we will notice a statement which explains that a long lever, or moment arm, produces a strong force while a short lever produces a weak force. By applying this principle it is, in fact, possible to create a half-twist jump in the straight position whilst suspended in mid-air. When the performer creates this twist his arm will be fully extended and perpendicular to the axis of rotation: in this case the longitudinal axis. The idea behind this is to construct as long a lever, or moment arm, as possible, which in turn will produce a strong force. When the arm is thrown across the body along this plane the body will turn in the opposite direction with an equivalent force per mass. In order to return the arm to its original position so that it may be thrown across the body once more, and yet at the same time prevent the body from returning to its original state, the arm must move along a different line. This is done by keeping the arm as close to the axis of rotation as possible on its return journey. When the arm is kept close to the body its leverage is greatly diminished since it is the perpendicular length to the axis of rotation which determines its strength. In this way the body will move through a greater number of degrees when the arm is thrown across the body than when the arm is returned to its original position. By continually swinging the arm round and round in this manner it is possible for the body to rotate around 180°. Because, as you can imagine, this method is so laborious and unsightly, we do not use it in trampolining—but it is just as well to be aware of what is happening when analysing other movements. For the straightforward plain jump with a twist, we do, therefore, take the twist straight from the bed from a *torque* action.

When performing twisting somersaults the body normally breaks the line of the axis of rotation either by being tucked, piked or hollowed and thus alleviating the performer of much of the problem of equal and opposite reaction. However, this problem is always with us and never completely obliterated. Forward somersaulting movements with twists are normally executed in the tucked and piked positions and so, for the sake of clarity, I will explain twisting movements in the piked position. Bearing in mind that all equal and opposite reaction must be minimized in order to gain as much benefit as possible from a swinging arm in twisting movements, we can base our reasoning on the lesson learned from twisting jumps. The best application of a lever is when it is perpendicular to the axis of rotation. At this point it is most effective because its extremity is further from the axis of rotation and, therefore, in its strongest position when applied. A weak leverage is where the throwing arm is kept close to the body and parallel to the axis of rotation. In piked twisting movements the body is out of line of the proposed axis of lateral rotation. This approximate axis about which the twist is to be executed runs through the back, out of the lower chest, through the centre of gravity of the body and then through the legs just above the knees (Fig. 11). The body is locked at the hips and

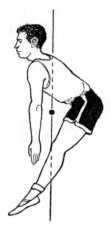

Fig. 11

thereby gives a fixed base upon which to create a twisting action. When an arm is thrown across the body as a means of setting the shoulder rotation, there is a reaction from the legs to move across in the opposite direction and so a *couple* is created. In order to try to obliterate this equal and opposite reaction, the arm is thrown in the direction of the knees and parallel to the longitudinal axis. It will mean that the arm-throw is not exactly along its most effective path, but this is more than compensated by the almost imperceptible amount of opposite reaction from the legs. Once the twist has been initiated, the body may then be straightened and the twisting action will continue through the whole of the body. The movement of straightening the body will bring its extremities, in this case the head, hips and feet, in line with the axis of the twist and, therefore, the whole lateral rotation will be accelerated.

The theory behind the action of creating a twist in the

hollowed-back position is the same as that for the piked twisting somersault. To minimize the amount of equal and opposite reaction the arm-throw must be along a line as near to and parallel to the axis about which the twist is going to centre. The longitudinal axis in this case runs along a line through the chest, the small of the back and from the back of the knees through the front of the shins. The direction of the arm-throw is over the shoulder and behind the head (Fig. 12). In order to get some idea

Fig. 12

as to the amount of opposite reaction to this arm-throw, stand behind a performer whilst he throws a hollowed-back somersault, a full twisting backward somersault, a double twisting backward somersault and any other multiple twisting backward somersault. The more force behind the throw, the greater amount the legs will move out of line from the longitudinal axis.

Although there has been a fantastic advance in the number and different types of twisting somersault movements, very little research has been carried out as to the real reasons that enable a somersaulting body to twist. There have been many theories put forward by people who believe that they know the reasons causing twists but so often even reputable lecturers on this subject have been proved wrong. Basically, their ideas have been the same, but it has been in the application of these ideas that the differences have arisen. Even in the way in which performers execute each theory there is a common factor which really causes the twist and whatever else happens is immaterial. This is where the mind and eyes can sometimes play tricks in interpreting what is actually happening.

Before we can understand what happens when a somersaulting body creates a twist, we must first look at the changes in body position that take place during this action. Basing our reasoning on the law of conservation of angular momentum, explained earlier, we are able to realize the common factor of all the twisting theories. When the body is rotating about a lateral axis whether in a straight, piked or tucked position, it is symmetrical either side of an imaginary line drawn through the head, centre of gravity and feet. Since both sides are equal, there will

Fig. 13

be a uniform speed of rotation. If only one side of the body was to be lengthened, or shortened, there would be an entirely different rate of velocity on that side which would also cause rotation about the longitudinal axis. A good example of this is to fix two wheels of unequal diametre to a common axle. When set in motion, besides rotating about each hub, there will also be rotation about a perpendicular axis somewhere along the axle near to the smaller wheel (Fig. 13). A performer executing a twisting somersault is very similar to this. There is rotation about the lateral axis (the axle) and also about the longitudinal axis (the perpendicular to the axle).

When analysing twisting somersaults, therefore, we must look for the fact that one half of the body on either side of the longitudinal axis most probably has a weaker moment of inertia. This asymmetrical body position can easily be obtained by use of the arms. By extending or bending one arm only there will automatically be a difference in the moments of inertia between the two sides of the body and, therefore, a difference in the angular velocity. Imagine any forward twisting somersault movement

Fig. 14

where the twist is created in the air. Having taken off from the bed, the body normally takes up an open pike, or half-lever position, with the arms symmetrically raised at approximately an angle of 45° to the rest of the body. As one arm is thrown across the body that shoulder as well as the arm is lower than on the other side of the body making the moments of inertia on either side different. This alone is enough to create angular momentum about the longitudinal axis. If the other arm is brought down behind the head the difference is still visible. By returning the body to a symmetrical state, the moments of inertia will be balanced and, therefore, any twist in the body from this method will be checked (Fig. 14).

When a performer takes a twisting movement straight from the bed then this rotation around the longitudinal axis will remain with the performer until another force acts upon it (Newton's Law of Inertia), such as landing on the bed again. Any rotary action that takes place as the result of two pairs of forces acting at the same time will be about an axis which is produced through the sum of these combined forces. This means that a third, entirely different, axis of rotation will be used throughout the movement.

It can be realized that there are different methods of creating twisting somersaults. Each method could be used separately or combinations of these together. I hope that I have given you something to think about so that whenever you see these movements being performed or are about to teach or coach them, you will try to analyse what is required with more understanding. I believe that much more research needs to be carried out on this subject before we will be completely satisfied with our theories

5

Basic Movements

The basic movements we teach comprise six different jumps and five different landing positions, excluding the feet. So far as the jumps are concerned there is no set order for tuition purposes since all take-offs and landings are from and to the feet. But because of the positions to be attained in the air the performers may find that they master them in the following order:

Tuck Jump. From take-off the performer should reach high into the air and just before obtaining his maximum height he should draw his knees tightly to his chest (Fig. 15). At the same

Fig. 15

time he should lean slightly forward extending his arms down the outside length of his lower legs. As the body begins to drop towards the bed again, the performer should stretch his body ready for the landing. This leaning forward as the knees are drawn up is another example of Newton's Third Law—'For every action there is an equal and opposite reaction.' Also, because the knees and trunk come forward there would be the reaction of the hips moving backward. The drawing-up of the knees takes place just before reaching maximum height so that an optical illusion is presented which makes it appear that the performer is still travelling upward after optimum height has been achieved. The arms are extended alongside the lower leg with the hands covering the ankles so that an aesthetic line may be shown rather than elbows sticking out when the shins are grasped by the hands.

Piked Straddle Jump. The take-off for each of the jumps is very similar in every case. The performer should always reach as high into the air as he can before commencing the movement. The legs are raised forward and upward and parted sideways at the same time. As in the Tuck Jump, the arms and trunk move downward to meet the legs (Fig. 16). If the arms are fully ex-

Fig. 16

tended when they are brought forwards and downwards from above the head to meet the legs, the raising of the legs will become easier. The reason for this is because by extending the arms a long, and therefore strong, leverage is set up. Newton's Third Law, you will remember, states that, 'For every action there is an equal and opposite reaction.' The term 'equal' here refers to equality in mass, weight, power, etc. By looking at our arms and legs it is not difficult to see that our legs easily outweigh our arms. Therefore, if the weight of our arms alone was used to counter-balance the weight of our legs there would be very little upward lift by the legs. It is very true to say that our trunk also moves forward to assist in this balance, but because of the position of our centre of gravity and the amount the body has to move backwards in the adjustment of body weight, only the upper part of the trunk counter-balances this leg action. Therefore, if we wish to execute this movement well, the legs must be raised to the horizontal position at least, and this will mean utilizing all the power we can muster from a long and powerful leverage created by fully extending the arms.

When the hands make contact with the legs in piked positions, we usually aim to rest the palms and fingers along the tops of the ankles so that a more tapered form is presented to onlookers. In America, however, there is a tendency to push the extended arms vertically between the legs as an alternative.

As the legs are lowered for the landing, the arms are raised upward again ready to continue with the normal arm swing in order to gain height for the next movement. The landing, as with *all* feet landings, will be with feet hip-width apart.

The raising of the legs in this jump will be slower than as for the Tucked Jump because of the longer, stronger leverage being used. This will mean that the legs, in the Pike Straddle Jump, will have to commence their upward journey slightly earlier than as for the Tucked Jump in order to pass through the required number of degrees (90°) by the time the body is ready to drop towards the bed once more. The raising of the legs to the side as much as possible will help the performer in the execution of this movement as well as making a true definition between this and the ordinary Piked Jump which so many competitors fail to show.

Piked Jump. The take-off is the same as for the Piked Straddle but this time the legs are drawn tightly together as they are raised upwards (Fig. 17). If the legs are not fully together throughout the movement it may be mistaken for a badly performed Piked Straddle. Similarly, a Piked Straddle where the legs are not wide enough apart could be mistaken for a badly performed Piked Jump. As the performer again drops towards the bed, the arms are raised upward so that they are positioned

78

ready to continue the arm swing in the normal manner. Many bouncers find that the Piked Straddle Jump is far easier than the ordinary Piked Jump and, therefore, I have described them in this order. The reason for this preference is that the state of a beginner's hamstrings at this stage of learning does not allow the range of suppleness which is required to perform the Piked Jump properly. By parting the legs the leverage becomes weaker.

Fig. 17

Forward and Backward Splits Jump. This movement is usually looked upon as a jump for the female followers of trampolining, although even amongst these there are very few who can perform it with the grace of the performer in the photograph. The take-off is the same as for all the previous jumps. As the performer soars upward she raises one leg forward and upward and the other leg backward and upward into a splits position. The arms can either be stretched, one forward and one backward, to counteract the legs or they may be extended sideways, thereby forming the pattern of a cross when viewed from above or below. The aim in both cases is to symmetrize the position. As the performer returns to the bed her arms are raised above her head into a position ready to continue the normal arm swing.

Half-twist Jump. For all twisting jumps in the straight position it is far better to execute the twist direct from the bed. By pushing against the bed with the feet and turning the upper half of the body in the direction of the required movement, a *torque* is created. As the performer rises and the feet lose contact with the bed, the twisting action will continue throughout the body

79

around the longitudinal axis. This twisting action will continue to take place for as long as the body is airborne. It is, therefore, most important that the right amount of twist required is gauged on take-off. The position of the arms throughout this movement is left entirely to the discretion of the performer. There are many variations, as can be seen from some of the examples shown here (Fig. 18). The main factors which must be borne in mind

Fig. 18

are that the arms must be kept as close to the axis of rotation as possible because any lengthening of the moment arm, or radius of gyration, will only decrease the angular velocity or speed of the twist. Also on the downward flight it is better to have the arms in a position above the head so that the full arm swing can be utilized to depress the bed on landing and, thereby, obtain a more efficient recoil.

Full-twist Jump. This will be the same as for the half-twist but more force will be applied from the feet into the bed in order to increase the amount of angular velocity. Remember that the amount of twist required must be determined on take-off. Because of this increase in velocity, the centrifugal force will also be stronger. This pulling outwards away from the axis of rotation often causes the performer to over-balance and, therefore, the greater the amount of angular velocity applied, the stronger

27. Keith Butler, British Professional Cycling champion in 1964 is amongst the top cyclists now using the Trampoline in training.

29. Brian Phelps, European Diving Champion in 1962 and Olympic Bronze Medallist in 1960, in action at the Crystal Palace National Recreation Centre.

28. Second pilot Lt. Col. Alexei Arkhipovich Leonov in space being watched by Commander of Spaceship VOSKHOD-2, Cosmonaut pilot Col. Pavel Ivanovich Belyaer.

30. George Nissen and Scott Carpenter at the Manned Spacecraft Center in Houston, Texas.

31. (*Left*) Linda Ludgrove has a work-out on the Trampoline under the watchful eye of her father.

32. (*Below, left*) The author, extreme right, coaching Brian Phelps during a training session for Britain's first full international team prior to leaving for Kiel, Germany, 1960.

33. (*Below, right*) Johnnie Ions of the Army Gymnastic Association performing during the trial for the international team match in Holland, 1963.

34. Britain's historic international team 1960. *Left to right:* Pete Quinney, Pat Winkle, Randall Bevan, Brian Phelps and Len Rapkins.

will be the pull away from the axis of rotation and a greater degree of control is required.

It is possible to create a twisting jump in the air but this can only take place when the body position is out of line from the axis of rotation, as from a piked or hollow-back position. The technique for creating twists in these positions is explained in the chapter on Mechanics. With twisting somersaults, the body is already somersaulting in one of these positions when the twist is introduced and, therefore, they are complementary to each other. In a twisting jump, however, the twist is usually executed in the straight position and any break in this line will cause a wriggle as the twist is produced. This will be aesthetically un-pleasing and, therefore, not advocated by trampolinists.

Seat Drop. We usually select the Seat Drop as the first move-ment to be taught after the straightforward feet-bounces for two reasons. One, because the movement at the initial stage is similar to something which is already known, i.e. sitting down in an armchair and, therefore, there is a certain carry-over. The second reason is because all of these basic drops are unnatural landings and if a beginner can appreciate, through something already experienced, that the landing on a trampoline is soft and safe then he should feel happier about landing on other parts of his body.

The performer should first be put in the position of the Seat Drop in the centre of the trampoline, so that a feeling of this correct posture may be appreciated. The legs should be together and fully extended with the toes pointed. The body should lean backward from the waist with the hands making contact with the bed about 6 in. behind the seat. Always make sure that the fingers point towards the feet. In this position the elbows will flex normally should a bad landing be executed. If the fingers are turned outwards or backward the elbows will be locked and a sharp pain may be experienced if too much weight is placed upon them.

The recoil from a trampoline is always along the same path as that which the mass travelled on its journey into the bed. Too many people try to perform a Seat Drop with the body at 90° to the legs or vertical to the bed with the result that the thrust from

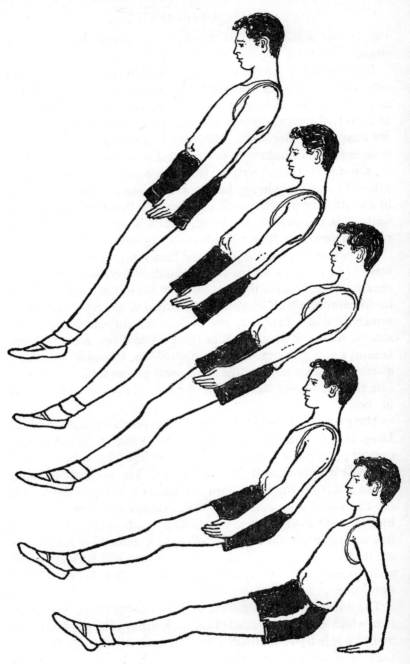

Fig. 19

the bed is directly upward. This was one of the original techniques and meant that to get back to the feet, the legs had to be bent underneath the body. Some of the old instructional films show top performers having to break form in this way in order to recover their feet. As we learned more about the techniques involved in trampolining, so the upper half of the body leant farther backward, putting increased weight on the hands. The thrust from the trampoline was now through the arms at an angle to the bed and a second-class leverage was being set up. The force was at one end (the hands); the weight in the middle (the body); and the pivot at the other end (the feet). In this new position the body naturally returned to the feet from the recoil and body form could be maintained. With all the basic drops it is quite unnecessary to bounce first in order to complete the movement satisfactorily. Far too many beginners are seen bouncing away ten or twelve times before trying the required drop. There is quite enough for the performer to think about with the movement itself. Trying to control the bounces before it only goes towards making the task in hand even more difficult. Simplicity itself is the key-word. Make the movements so simple that anyone can achieve success. People are only too ready to repeat anything with which they can associate success. So remember, all basic drops should be executed from an ordinary standing position first. It can be done and the rate of progress will be increased.

Another faulty technique which is sometimes used is that where the performer takes up the Seat Drop position whilst at the top of his height. On landing the feet are invariably slightly later in making contact with the bed than the rest of the body. The result is that a Kaboom action is set up and the body rotates backwards giving no chance of regaining the feet. The most reliable way to execute a proper Seat Drop is to make sure that during the upward flight the body is kept fully extended. By the time the performer has reached the summit of his height, the toes should be pointing towards the end cables. Because the toes are pointing towards the end cables it will mean that the performer will have rotated very slowly in this straight position. The body will remain perfectly balanced because of the equal

83

and opposite amounts the body rotates either side of the vertical. Throughout the descent the toes should remain pointing toward the end cables. In order to do this the body will begin to pike the correct amount and at the right speed so that by the time contact with the bed is made, a perfect Seat Drop position will be formed every time.

Knee Drop. We normally follow the Seat Drop with the Knee Drop because the performer does not have to alter his body position very much from the normal feet-bouncing attitude. As with all new landing positions, put the performer in the correct posture before he attempts it for himself. If this can be coupled with a demonstration at the same time, all the better. The body should be upright with all the weight over the knees. The toes should be together and the knees hip-width apart, forming a triangular base for stability. In this way, any sideways cast can easily be corrected, whereas with the knees together the body has very little control. If on landing the performer sits back on his heels, then this bending at the knees absorbs the recoil from the bed and great difficulty is experienced in trying to rebound to the feet. On the other hand, if the hips are pushed too far forward outside the line of the body, then a very sharp pain will be felt. The reason for this is that on contact with the bed the rate of inertia of the knees is slowed somewhat, while the head and shoulders are still travelling at their original speed. Something has to make way for this moving mass and so the hips are forced even further forward, causing the vertebrae to meet and pinch the inter-vertebral cartilage. Although this is a sharp pain, the effects wear off very quickly and the performer is able to continue bouncing almost immediately.

From the standing position the performer should be told to push into the bed and just lift his heels behind himself until the shins are parallel to the bed. The position can be held for the landing and maintained until the recoil lifts the performer clear of the bed. The lower leg may then be lowered and the landing can be made to feet in the normal manner.

Apart from the two positional faults that were mentioned earlier a beginner may either lean forward in front of the point of take-off, with the result that the recoil will throw him forward, or he may pivot backward on his toes when returning to feet. The correction in the first instance is to instil into the mind of the performer that the body weight must be directly over the knees, hence the name given to this particular movement. In the second instance the performer must remain in the kneeling position until he has rebounded at least 2 ft. above the bed.

Hands-and-Knee Bounce. Once again, first put the beginner in the correct position. Obviously, as its name implies, the performer needs to take up an attitude on both hands and knees. The back should not be parallel to the bed, as many people think, but sloping towards the feet (Fig. 20). On this occasion,

Fig. 20

the performer may sit back on his heels. He is going to land on the bed already in this position and, therefore, there will be no flexion to kill the bounce. The hands touch the bed just in front of the knees and in this position the body weight lands in a concentrated area, giving an even rebound. I have seen quite a few people executing this drop by trying to land on the bed with a flat back. This means that the hands make contact with the bed

85

at some distance from the knees, causing two distinct points of impact. The result is two recoils which so often force the bouncer to perform a 'Bucking Bronco' act. Also, with the two extremities being checked on landing, the middle of the back is apt to buckle, causing pain.

Front Drop. There is a natural lead-in to the Front Drop from a Hands-and-Knees Drop because this is the first attitude we adopt. By starting from hands and knees the centre of gravity of the body is brought close to the bed. In this way what could prove to be a frightening experience is made simpler. Let the performer lie on the bed as if he was sunbathing in the South of France, with the body and legs fully extended (the toes pointing towards the end cables) and the arms fixed so that the hands are placed just under the face with finger-tips touching. The landing must be made along the full length of the front of the body, and the length of the forearms and hands. The flatter the landing, the more comfortable for the performer. Females especially try to hold their faces up away from the bed; this is only asking for trouble because if the legs touch the bed first the recoil will throw them upward, forcing the face downward at speed. Bounce on the hands and knees to the count of three and then extend the legs backward to land in the Front Drop position. By extending the legs only, the majority of the body weight remains in its original position over the bed and just drops straight downward for the landing. If a performer tries to extend the body by diving forward, the mass of body weight will slide along the bed, causing burns on the skin especially to the nose, elbows and knees.

Back Drop. This movement is usually taught last since not only is it an unnatural landing, but also because the performer cannot see where he is going. The area of the back to be landed upon is made known to the performer either by the coach outlining this with his hands through putting pressure on the region or by putting the performer in the position on the bed. The next thing is to get the performer to make the correct landing safely.

The performer should stand in the middle of the bed with his feet hip-width apart and his arms folded. The hips should be pushed forward as far as they will go making sure that the knees do not bend and that a perfect balance is maintained throughout. The head should be held in a forward position so that the eyes may look at the folded arms the whole time. Holding this position the performer should just fall backward. If this correct attitude is preserved, a perfect Back Drop will result. However, it is not uncommon practice for a beginner to hold form right until the last second and then 'sit' on the bed. This bending at the hips as the body weight falls backward invariably causes a landing on the point of the seat which in turn sends a whip-lash along the spine to the head. The head is jolted backward and a sharp pain is felt at the back of the neck. Should this happen, confidence must be instilled into the performer by the coach either verbally or by placing a hand behind the performer's seat, as he falls backward, making sure that the back lands first. Emphasis must be laid on the lifting of the hips high out of the way of the bed. If the hips are lifted correctly, then they cannot get in the way when landing.

Another method is to get the performer to stand on one leg with his other leg lifted in front of himself. The coach may take hold of this raised leg and elevate it higher so as to guide the performer on to his back.

The other, almost involuntary, reaction is to save oneself by placing the hands down first or by executing a Judo break-fall. It is for this reason that the arms are folded to keep them away from the bed. Should a performer still insist on breaking from the folded arms position then he should be given something to hold in front of his body such as a light football or a plimsoll. Because he is actually holding on to something there is more of a reluctance to let go.

As soon as two basic drops have been mastered they should be linked together in swingtime and then each new movement included until a neat routine of these basic drops is being performed. The first linking movement, therefore, is *Seat to Knees* and *Knees to Seat*. Because the Knee Drop requires a vertical landing we usually begin with this in the combination move. The Knee Drop is performed in exactly the same way outlined earlier. As the bouncer rises from the bed he should lean backward and kick his legs forward to the Seat Drop position. The performer must remember not to lean backward until he is on the rise, otherwise the smoothness and ease of performance will deteriorate.

The secret of the *Seat Drop to Front Drop* is in pushing the head down to the feet. Since the body is leaning backward with the Seat Drop, the weight is on the hands, and all the push from the hands, therefore, should be used to throw the upper half of the body forward. The head is held down and the legs tucked through and extended to the rear. The landing position is the same as for a normal Front Drop.

The *Front Drop to Back Drop* is a movement which many people find to be the most difficult. The reason is usually because the head is thrown backward, hoping to cause rotation, when all that happens is that the legs rise at the other end because of the equal and opposite reaction and the performer just hangs in the air. The correct method for performing this movement is to push and pull the hands under the body, keeping the head still and concentrating on lifting the hips forward and upward. Once the body has been set in rotation it should be tucked to accelerate the whole movement. The performer could try actually landing in the tucked position until the feeling of the movement is appreciated and then gradually open out before landing.

The combination of basic drops which is used more than any other is: Knees to Seat to Front to Back. The reason for this can quite easily be realized by thinking of the body-weight position for each landing and the action of the suspension system. If you stand at one end of the bed and bounce up and down you will notice that the cables at that end are being fully extended whilst at the other end there is hardly any movement. The throw will also be to catapult you towards the middle. Therefore, let us analyse this combination. The one movement that must have a vertical landing with no throw is the Knee Drop. By leaning backward on take-off it is easy to fall naturally into a Seat Drop. Because the body is leaning backward the weight is on the back half of the bed which will automatically catapult it forward. Add to this the fact that the hands are also pushing the body forward at the same end and you can see that forward rotation to a Front Drop is the obvious next position. Conversely, the body weight and hands are now in the forward half of the bed so that the resultant thrust will be backward. The only basic drop left, therefore, is the Back Drop. This appreciation of the body-weight position, the throw from the bed and the momentum already in the body are the basis of compiling good competition routines that flow together smoothly.

6

Rotational Progressions

Although backward rotations are much easier to execute than forward rotations, we usually begin with teaching the forward rotation because the performer can see where he is going on take-off, and this is usually the difficulty which has to be overcome.

Forward Somersault. The first thing is to sort out whether the performer has the ability to turn over without rolling on to one shoulder. Should this occur, then you have problems, but more about this later when I shall give you some tips on trying to cure this fault.

Let the performers stand at one end of the trampoline with one foot either side of the red line which runs along the length of the bed. By keeping this red line central to the line of the body it is easy to see if the performer rolls to one side. Provided that there is no deviation from the straight roll, the next stage is from hands and knees. The performer should drop on to hands and knees, lift the hips until they are above the hands and then tuck the head under to make a landing on to the back. This movement should then be repeated from a knee drop, only without using the hands. Still from the knees, the performer should use the hips to get more rotation and continue to somersault over to a seat drop. The next stage is to get more hip lift for rotation and grasp just below the knees for a good tucked position, thereby accelerating the rotation, and try to land on the feet.

In the early days people used to suffer from the knees coming into contact with the face on landing, causing great discomfort.

Today we advocate that on take-off the soles of the feet should be placed together, which will cause the knees to be spread apart. This gives a void space into which the head can enter safely on landing. Performing the movement this way means that the landing will be made on the outer borders of the feet, if still in the tucked position. Although this may seem dangerous, no injury will be caused because the bed will mould itself around the shape of the feet. If the performer can see his way round and is able to stand up as he lands, all the better. The reason for taking the whole movement from the knees is to lower the centre of gravity of the performer and thereby allow a greater margin for error.

For a final stage, to give encouragement and confidence, I suggest that the coach stands on the left side of the performer with his right hand holding the performer's left. If the coach's palm faces upward and the performer's downward, the latter's arm will not be twisted on landing. Another technique which I use is to grip the performer's left thumb between my index finger and middle finger, whilst in the hand grip. In this way, when the hands are damp with perspiration, a stronger grip is obtained which prevents the hands slipping apart. Having gained confidence in this way, the performer can then make an attempt at the full movement with the coach standing at the front end of the trampoline.

When someone continually rolls over to one side, the fault stems almost without doubt from a lack of confidence in turning over safely. This confidence must be given to the performer, somehow. There seem to be two alternatives which work. One is to take the performer to a stage of Hands and Knees Drop to handstand, holding the head back to look at the bed for as long as possible before tucking the head under. The other alternative is to take the performer through the whole movement, first having let him experience turning over on his own once or twice, even with a roll. Through continual practice, this first method, gradually getting a faster rotation and taking the hands from the bed earlier, will allow the performer to see where he is for most of the way round. The safer he feels, the more he will put into the movement and the barrier may be overcome in this manner. The supporting grip for the second method should be the same as mentioned earlier. Just bounce together first to get the rhythm. This enables the coach to feel the reaction of the performer and allows the performer to accustom himself to the experience of bouncing with another person. When the coach decides that the time is right he should inform the performer that the next time the movement will be executed. The coach should then count to three, killing his own bounce and kipping the performer on the third contact with the bed. The coach's left hand should support the back of the performer and help to rotate him throughout the movement. When the coach's left hand has passed under his right hand it returns to the front to support the chest in case of an overthrow.

A One and a Quarter Somersault to Front Drop is the next progression in forward rotation. Knowing the ability of your performers has a great bearing on the methods you utilize in teaching new movements. In the case of the one and a quarter forward somersault it is quite safe, in many cases, to explain the movement and the performer will execute this without any difficulty. However, with the more timid performer it may mean returning to a Knee Drop take-off and rotating through 450° to a Hands-and-Knee Drop. Because the performer is landing in a semi-tucked position, the speed of rotation will continue from take-off through to the landing. When the bed is clearly sighted the body may be fully extended to the correct Front Drop position. With confidence the full movement can be taken from the feet.

A One and Three-quarter Forward Somersault. Naturally the trampolinist does not perform a one and a half forward somersault as this would mean landing on the head which in turn leads to a loss of interest in the sport! The next movement then is the one and three-quarter forward somersault. This, I feel, can best be learned from a diving board into water. The movement and techniques are the same until it comes to the landing. From the diving board, the performer is able to show a good snappy opening-out from the fast rotation, which is very necessary. The last part of the movement is again what is required by the trampolinist; descending towards the water, or trampoline, head

92

first in the extended position. From the diving board it does not hurt if the performer enters slightly short of, or slightly past, the required perpendicular. On the trampoline the performer must either land in the Front Drop position or past the vertical to a Back Drop landing. Anywhere between these two can be rather disconcerting. Another method of learning this movement is in a belt attached to an overhead rig. The rope-handler can stop the performer as he is descending head-first towards the bed, giving him a chance to see where he is. Then, by being gradually lowered to a handstand position, the performer is able to orientate himself so as to know how far from the bed he needs to tuck under to land on his back safely. The most important aspect is that the performer knows where he is at any time throughout any movement. It is surprising the number of bouncers in the past who have learnt this movement backward. That is, they have just spun into a rotation on take-off and held on to the spin in a tucked position until a back landing is made. In this way the movement is executed by timing only and can be painful if insufficient rotation is set up at the beginning. The earlier the performer can see what is happening, the safer the movement becomes. This one and three-quarter somersault is used more in swingtime routine work than any other forward somersaulting movement. It is, therefore, worth perfecting and retaining among your list of stunts for routine work. Another factor is the important role this movement plays in the learning of fliffus movements.

The *Double Forward Somersault* is not usually performed in routine work because the opening-out to land is a blind movement and, therefore, a very difficult one from which to work into another stunt. The safest way of executing a double somersault for the first time is in a belt. Because of this blind opening it is very easy to pitch over forward or, in anticipation of this, to come out early to an arched back landing. In the belt any mistakes made on take-off or in the air can easily be rectified by the rope handler. As a single stunt, like so many other things, it is there and is a task to be conquered.

The *Two and a Quarter Forward Somersault*, like the double somersault is not usually performed in routine work. Although

93

a greater number of degrees is passed through, allowing the performer to see the bed on landing, it is the landing which is the difficulty. To execute a Front Drop from a fast rotating movement often causes anxiety to the performer as to how he will land. For this reason a number of people check too much with the hands on landing, which creates an incorrect position. Once again, being a flat position with forward momentum there is very little one can perform out of this movement and it is, therefore, very rarely seen in competition work.

The *Two and Three-quarter Forward Somersault*, although tariff-wise it is a very useful movement, is not used as much as the one and three-quarter somersault by performers. The most important reason for this is that the latter movement has many uses in the learning of the different types of fliffes. However, when the two and three-quarter is performed well it gives greater power on the recoil for performing various Ball-out movements. It is possible to continue adding another 90° rotation to the last stunt but apart from the individual tariff value there is little point. Always remember that forward rotational movements to feet require timing and a blind landing.

It is possible to create rotation about a lateral axis from the different basic drops and so continuing with the forward rotation we are able to perform these next movements.

Front Cody or Front Kaboom. The Cody movement was named after Dale Cote of Los Angeles who just happened to be passing when someone was leading up to the backward one and a quarter somersault from the stomach. Dale was asked to stand in as a spotter while the performer went for the complete stunt. The attempt was successful and in his rejoicing the performer asked the spotter his name and decided to call the movement a Cote, or Cody as it is more commonly known. The Cody, which is a somersaulting action from a Front Drop, can be performed either forward or backward. A three-quarter somersault is executed in the forward direction and a one and a quarter somersault when rotating backward. A kaboom action is when two parts of the body make contact with the bed consecutively, causing rotation. This rotation will come from the later contact because the body will have become airborne through the first

94

contact with the bed and, therefore, there will be no resistance to the second recoil. As a Front Drop landing is being made, the knees are pressed into the bed, often with the assistance of the lower leg being bent backward at the knee. This extra pressure results in the legs being thrown upward on the recoil and forward rotation is achieved. It is also possible to beat the feet down onto the bed as the body is rising and thereby create a 'kaboom' action. Since the feet were the last part of the body to make contact with the bed, this end rebounds into the air and, again, forward rotation is the result.

The progressions for this forward rotating movement are to get a good Front Drop with the feet banging on the bed forcibly so that the recoil from the feet can really be appreciated. As the performer gains confidence, a handstand position can be reached so that he can see the bed all the way and estimate the required amount of rotational force to turn him over to his back safely. From here onward it is purely a case of getting good timing with the kaboom action and tucking tightly to get right over to feet. To get further assistance into this movement, a gaining one and a quarter forward somersault should be executed as the lead-in. The take-off from the stomach then has the advantage of the forward momentum which has been built up from the one and a quarter somersault.

Ball-out. This is the name given to a one and a quarter forward somersault from a Back Drop take-off. To get the feeling of rotating forward from this position we need to think of the mechanical principles of a first-class lever. If the performer lies in the Back Drop position it is easy to appreciate the leverage system. The trunk and main bulk of the body is the weight; the hips act as the fulcrum and the legs the actual lever bar. If the body were to remain braced in this position and downward power applied to the feet, then the weight, or trunk, would be raised. The performer is able to do just this by swinging the legs downward under his own muscle power. The rest of the body, being attached to the legs, will be swung over to a Front Drop position quite easily. Many people try to raise the upper trunk in this movement but since no power can come from this end other than the actual landing and recoil, there is a struggle and a poor execution results. By swinging the legs vigorously downward and coming over to a Front Drop first, the performer is able to see the amount of rotation he has and also orientate himself. With a little more height and a harder leg swing, the performer should then tuck his head under as he sees the bed. This tucking under or slight piking action will accelerate the rotation and a safe landing on to the back can be made. By increasing the swinging power of the legs the full movement to feet can be achieved. Should there be any difficulty it is most probably because the person is throwing low and does not have the rotational height to complete the movement. In this case the legs of the performer should be brought farther over his face making a more acute angle with the body. The leg swing will then be upward first, before swinging round and down. This upward swing will cause the body to be pushed farther into the bed with the resultant higher recoil.

Backward Somersault. Some people commence teaching this movement by first getting the performer to execute what is known as a *Back Pull-over*. For this the performer stands at one end of the bed, jumps into the air to a tightly held tucked position and lands on his feet and seat still in this position. So long as the tucked position is maintained throughout, the resultant reaction will be a backward rotation to feet. Other people believe that because the performer does not actually do anything there is no carry-over to the actual backward somersault. It is for you to decide whether the movement would be an aid for your students or not. The backward somersault is a movement which so many people want to execute before they have really mastered the control of the bed. The result is usually a travelling somersault from one end of the bed to the other. To eliminate any such travel we always teach this move with the coach or supporter on the bed with the performer.

The first stage is for the supporter to stand behind the performer with one hand, usually the stronger, at the back of the neck and the other hand on the performer's waist. Then bouncing together to get the rhythm and timing, the supporter should audibly count to three so as to give the performer some idea as to when he will be required to execute the movement. On in-

35. The England and West German competitors renew old acquaintances in Wageningen 1963. *Left to right:* Yvonne Horne, Helmut Riehle, Lila Webb, Dieter Schulz, Gisela Germar, Johnnie Ions, Gerda Schmidt, Horst Schlindwein, Joyce Thomas, Dave Smith, Gisela Haferkamp and Chris Netherton.

36. The place winners congratulate each other on the rostrum. *From left to right:* Gary Erwin, 2nd, Danny Millman, 1964 World Champion and Dave Smith, Consolation Bracket winner.

37. The best in the World receive their acclaim. *From left to right:* Lynda Ball, 2nd, Judy Wills, 1964 World Champion and Marijke van den Boogard, Consolation Bracket winner.

38. Dave Smith (Hove) performing a Rudolph during the First World Championships 1964.

39. Chris Netherton of England performing during the First World Championships 1964.

40. The teams line up. *From left to right, back row:* Werner Loer, Tony Pickup, Peter Quinney, Chris Netherton, Horst Schlindwein, Mike Williams, Helmut Riehle, Johnnie Ions, Les Kinnear, the author. *Front row:* Rob Walker, Dave Smith, John Newton, Michael Budenberg, Werner Willig and Manfred Haase, 1964.

41. (*Left*) John Newton performing in the Empire Pool Stadium during the Great Britain *v.* West Germany match, 1964.

42. (*Below*) Lynda Ball, Barbara John and Anne Goddard after the finals of the Ladies' Championships, 1965.

structions from the supporter, the performer should raise his eyes to the ceiling or sky, lifting his head rather than *throwing* it backward. When done properly, the performer should be able to do this on the spot without any travel. The coach should stand behind the performer, supporting him and all the time checking any inclination to throw backward. The indentation in the bed made by the coach standing behind the bouncer may automatically cause the performer to lean backward. Therefore, as soon as the bouncer has some control over the situation the coach should stand at the end of the trampoline. The second stage is for the arms to be swung upward and shoulder-width apart with the palms of the hands facing together. The hands should reach no higher than eye level. Instead of looking to the ceiling or sky, the performer can now watch his hands in preparation for later progressions and the full movement. The next stage is for the performer to raise his hips upward and slightly forward until his body is as near as possible to being parallel to the bed. It is better to have the hips raised beyond the parallel rather than not having reached this position. The coach supports in the same manner, one hand behind the neck and the other hand moving from the waist to right under the seat to give the best means of support. As the performer descends to replace his feet on to the bed, the coach's hand under the seat is lowered gently at the same time as the upper hand behind the neck is pushed forward at a corresponding speed, in order to rotate the performer safely to the upright position. The upper arm supporting the neck must always be kept straight throughout these movements otherwise the coach will find great difficulty in supporting efficiently. Following on from here, stage four requires the performer to snap into a tucked position after having reached the layout position parallel to the bed. The performer must watch his knees being raised into his hands all the time, thereby keeping his head in line with his body. This movement must be fast since the performer must still return to his original position as outlined in the last stage. When the coach is satisfied that there is sufficient rotation evident and that the layout position is being shown first, he can then prepare to support for the full movement. With the aid of a towel around the performer's waist, the coach should now stand on the bed at the bouncer's side. The best position is with the stronger hand holding the ends of the towel and the free hand to the front of the performer. The coach should again count to *three*, killing his own bounce for stability and assisting the performer with a kip. As the performer pushes from the bed, raising his hips upwards, the coach's free hand engages behind the bouncer's thighs to assist in rotating him safely. As the coach's arms cross each other, the free hand is brought forward again to grasp the upper arm of the performer to steady him. After a few somersaults performed in this manner the towel can be dispensed with and the supporter's hand is all that is required. Standing in the same supporting position, the coach's stronger hand is placed at the base of the performer's spine. A few pats with this hand to give the performer confidence and let him know someone is there and he is ready for what seems to be a big step. Should the performer's mind go blank and forget all that he has been taught, or in his anxiety to complete the movement there is a throw backward, this supporting hand at the base of the spine can push the hips forward to counteract any lean, and continue its pressure upwards to make certain there is sufficient rotation for safety. Once the performer has overcome this stage there should be no danger. As a precaution, however, the coach should stand at the end of the trampoline, either on the bed or on the frame, ready to step in should his assistance be required. Once the performer has turned over, the possible landings have all been covered by basic drops: Hands-and-Knees Drop; Feet; Seat Drop and Back Drop. Practice will give confidence, and confidence success.

To perform a backward somersault in the piked position the feet must be thrust upwards vigorously with the legs fully extended and the hips following. This movement will look neater if the hands grasp the back of the legs just *below the knees*. Pulling in at the back of the knees is apt to cause the knees to bend as a closer piked position is being sought.

With a completely hollowed-back somersault, the arms and chest should be lifted as high as possible, but still allowing sufficient hip action to create enough angular momentum for the somersault. The arms should be left in their upward position until the upper half of the body is approximately parallel to the bed. The arms should then be thrown downward, placing the hands on the front of the thighs. This throwing action will create an opposite reaction from the legs and cause them to lift more. Bringing the arms from above the head will also shorten the radius of gyration and accelerate the movement.

Lazy Back or Three-quarter Back Somersault. Because of the safety factor of landing correctly in the Front Drop position, this movement is always taught after the back somersault from feet-to-feet has been mastered. The best method of learning this movement is to slow down the rotational force of a complete back somersault right from take-off so that the landing is made on hands and knees. As the performer sees the bed prior to landing on his hands and knees, the body should be fully extended so that the Front Drop landing can be made. If too much or too little rotational force is apparent, then the performer is able to continue landing on hands and knees until confident to do otherwise. Gradually the complete somersault can be opened until the whole movement is in the layout position.

Back Somersault to Seat Drop. This used to be known as a one and a quarter somersault until it was pointed out that the upper half of the body was still perpendicular to the bed and, therefore, had only turned through 360°. To perform this movement the bouncer should hold on to the back somersault just a little longer until he sees that the feet have passed beyond their normal landing position. The legs should then be extended and the feet guided along the length of the bed keeping them as low as possible. On landing, the momentum will be backward and so the arms must be prepared to take the pressure. This is one of the times when the fingers need to be pointing in the direction of the feet to save any discomfort.

Back One and a Quarter to Back Drop. Again, the performer should hold on to the rotation even longer than mentioned for the last stunt, so that the legs can be sharply extended and the toes pointed to a position approximately 3 ft. above the trampoline. If the legs are held any higher a backward Pull-over is likely to result. The landing should be as for an ordinary Back Drop.

99

Double Backward Somersault. This is not as difficult a movement as the name may at first imply. The performer can see his way out of this quite easily, but even so I suggest that it is first performed in the belt. The build-up is normally a standing one and a quarter somersault first to get the right amount of rotational force on take-off, and as with the other backward somersaults, the arms should reach high with the hips thrusting through to create a fast somersault. The emphasis should be on driving the shins upward, rather than the knees, so that the tail end of the seat is also swung round and upward. By bringing the legs up soon after take-off, the somersaulting action is executed on the way up, giving more time for opening out and preparing for the landing. If the preliminary stages have been well established and the standing one and a quarter somersault can be executed easily, then there should be very little difficulty in performing the double. With a bounce to give the extra height to pass over the one and a quarter stage, four safe landings are presented; Hands-and-Knees—Feet—Seat-and Back. Invariably the performer is apt to over-throw the rotation rather than under-throw it, causing a roll over to back on landing. Again, practice and confidence will bring forth success.

One and Three-quarter Somersault. Because of the Front Drop landing this is more difficult than the double backward somersault. The lead-up stages are similar to those used in learning the lazy backward somersault, the exception being that the Hands-and-Knees Drop comes in the second somersault. With the powerful momentum which will still be with the performer on landing and the height from the bed that the head will be at this point, I again advise the use of the belt. As the performer becomes aware of his speed of rotation and position he will be able to straighten out for the correct Front Drop landing.

When trampolinists reach this stage of performance, the next backward movement is the *Triple Somersault.* The other intermediate movements, to Seat and Back Drop, are of no use to this person. Obviously this movement *must* be learnt in a belt. No matter how confident the performer is, or how fast his rotational speed, one slip and an uncomfortable landing could be the result With this movement the legs must be brought up-

100

ward and inward as soon as possible after the rotational power has been initiated from the bed. During the first two somersaults the head should be held forward to the knees in order to accelerate the angular velocity. It is only after two and a quarter somersaults have been executed that the performer needs to throw his head back to prepare for the landing.

Back Cody. As mentioned before, a Cody is a somersaulting action from a Front Drop. In the case of the Back Cody, a one and a quarter somersault is performed. The lead-up stages are: firstly, Front Drop to Back Drop; then Front Drop to Back Drop followed by a backward Pull-over to feet. The emphasis throughout must be on a good push from the bed with the hands and a strong and fast pull-through of the hips. The coach can easily tell when the performer is ready to be taken over through the full movement. From here onward there are three methods of supporting. The first is for the coach to 'kip' the performer just before he lands, giving him more height and, therefore, more time to complete the movement. Initially, the performer should still just turn over from Front Drop to Back Drop to make sure that the timing is right. The performer then knows what to expect and the resultant height achieved can be appreciated by both the coach and the performer. The coach should stand on the frame with one foot just making contact with the bed, riding its rise and fall to maintain the rhythm. His stronger hand will usually correspond with his stronger leg and, therefore, this side of his body will be towards the performer. The most advantageous position for supporting in this manner is for the coach to face in the same direction as the performer. The arm to be used for turning the performer then has a greater range of movement.

As the Front Drop landing is being made, the coach should place his full weight on to the foot resting on the bed, making a deep depression. Then, lifting this weight quickly from the bed, the performer would get the full benefit of this double impetus. Once the performer has left the bed the coach can step in and support by pushing and turning the performer at the back of his legs. It is possible for the coach's arm to remain in contact with the back of the performer's legs throughout the whole movement in one long sweeping action. As the performer lands on

101

his feet the coach should grasp his upper arm once again to steady the landing.

Another method of supporting for this movement is very similar to the one mentioned above, the exception being that two people act as supporters instead of one. The two supporters stand on the frame, one on either side of the performer. It is essential that these supporters are experienced in the art of kipping performers since their combined timing has to be exact. If one were to depress the bed slightly after the other, the whole recoil would be lost and the performer would land on a dead bed. They must also step on to the bed at the same time and support in the same manner as otherwise they could get in each other's way.

The third method is to have the performer in the belt and harness. One supporter would handle the ropes whilst the second supporter would turn the performer as described above.

Double Back Cody. The progressions would be to perform one and a quarter Back Codies to Back Drop, increasing the amount of rotation until the arms have to be flung backward to lengthen the radius of gyration and thereby slow down the movement to stop the performer from landing on his head. From here onward the supporting methods are the same as for a single Back Cody according to the ability and confidence of the performer.

Side Somersault. This is not usually performed in competition routines but is an interesting movement which is included in the Proficiency Award scheme and the Coaching Award schemes of the British Trampoline Federation. Therefore, one needs to know how to coach and perform it. The performer should stand in the middle of the bed facing the side, with the coach standing behind him. The grip, imagining that the performer is going to rotate to the right, is with the back of the coach's left hand on the performer's right hip and his right arm crossed over his left arm so that the right hand can hold the performer's left hip. Do not worry if the left hand is not actually gripping the right hip. Seeing that the rotation is to the right it is the left hip which has to be raised and the coach is in a position to do this if necessary. Whenever manually supporting a performer, always bounce together to get the rhythm before attempting the movement. The

102

coach should count to *three*, killing his bounce on the third landing as usual. The performer should be instructed to watch a fixed point on the trampoline, usually the sleeve into which the roller-stand engages, and not to lose sight of this throughout the movement. On the count of *three*, the performer should throw his left hip to the left and upwards, the coach supporting all the way. As the rotation is made, the performer will roll around the supporter's left hand so that on landing the left hand is now in the correct position to give support and the right hand is only a guide. There is usually an inclination to perform a backward movement rather than sideways. If this is the case get the performer to push his right shoulder forward during the movement and this, you will find, is usually the cure.

Turntable. A number of people tend to forget that this is actually a sideways somersault action and not a twist. The lead-up stages are to get the bouncer to perform a Front Drop followed by a horizontal tucked position and then open out back to the Front Drop landing again. The tendency is to push against the bed and raise the head on the recoil, causing a rotation of the body and the performer to land on his knees. The natural recoil from the bed should be enough to raise the body clear of the trampoline and, therefore, the hands should refrain from pushing the body upward. As the knees are brought forward to execute the tucked position, the head and shoulders should also be pushed under to meet the knees. In this way there should be equal movement from both ends of the body and no rotation set up. The landing back to the Front Drop will then be quite easy. The next stage is to get the performer to push against the bed in the opposite direction to that of his rotation. This pushing against the bed must take place as the performer's body is depressing the bed. Full weight must be behind the thrust. Again, the natural recoil from the trampoline is sufficient to lift the performer clear of the bed and, therefore, all his energy should be used in initiating the rotation about the dorso-ventral axis. Should the performer get a slight rotation about the longitudinal axis also, it is because his hands are remaining in contact with the bed too long when the rotation is initiated. An oral correction of this should be quite sufficient.

7

Twisting Progressions

The first practice for twisting progressions is to perform all the basic drops with twists. The safest way is to perform what is already known first, i.e. the basic drop followed by the half-twist. These are again performed in the same order as the basic drops were first learnt.

Seat Drop, Half-twist. From the Seat Drop push the body upward and at the same time push slightly more from one hand, turning the shoulders in the opposite direction. This will be sufficient to make the performer turn through 180° about this longitudinal axis.

Knee Drop, Half-twist. From the Knee Drop swing both arms upward and over one shoulder. The upper half of the body should turn in the same direction so that a torque is created. As soon as the knees leave the bed the whole body will complete the half-twist.

Front Drop, Half-twist. From the Front Drop, push downward and against the bed very vigorously in the opposite direction to the required twist. The downward push will rotate the body back to feet and the sideways force will rotate the body about the longitudinal axis. As the body rises from the bed, the head and shoulders should be turned hard in the direction of the twist.

Back Drop, Half-twist. As the body rises from the Back Drop, one arm and shoulder should be pushed across the body in the direction of the required twist. Since the body is in a piked position the top half of the trunk will twist against the lower

104

half. Then as the body straightens the twist will be completed.

Having experienced these movements with twist on the way out of the basic drop, the twist should now be executed before the basic landings.

Half-twist to the Knees. The movement requires an upright landing and therefore nothing in the preliminary half-twist must distract from this. A normal vertical jump with half-twist must be performed first and then, just before the landing, the heels should be raised backward to allow a usual Knee Drop to be executed.

Half-twist to Seat. The remaining drops all require a certain amount of body rotation about the lateral axis and for this reason the performer is made to think. For the normal Seat Drop, the legs were swung forward and the upper half of the body inclined backward. Now, with the half-twist before this drop the movement is reversed. The performer should reach forward and upward at about 30° on take-off, twisting the shoulders around the longitudinal axis at the same time. Because of the half-twist, this forward lean will now be transferred to a backward lean which is the required landing for a Seat Drop.

Half-twist to Front. Where as, in the normal Front Drop, the legs were swung backward, this time they are raised forward to an imaginary point approximately 2 ft. above the bed. At this point the whole length of the body should be at an angle of 45° to the bed. The body begins its twist around the longitudinal axis immediately on take-off, although this twist is very slight. At the top of the height only a quarter of a full twist (90°) should have been completed and the performer should still be watching his feet. As the descent is made, the head and body should turn to face the bed in preparation for the landing. The body must be fully stretched throughout this movement.

Half-twist to Back. Again the whole movement is reversed. Instead of the lower half of the body being raised forward it is pushed backward. In actual fact a normal Front Drop take-off is the ideal beginning. It is the twisting action that then seems to be the difficulty. There are two ways in which I have found success in teaching this movement. The first is to take-off as for a

Front Drop with one arm extended pointing towards the bed. As the performer descends towards the bed he calls out, 'There's the bed.' Then, swinging the arm, still fully extended sideways across his body, he points to the coach standing at the side saying, 'There's the coach.' If the arm is kept fully extended all the time and pushed across the body forcibly there should be no reason why this method should not work.

The second method is to place something soft, such as a handkerchief, sock or screwed-up piece of paper, on the bed after the performer has taken off for his Front Drop. The object should be placed in a position where the performer can swing an arm across the bed to sweep it off the trampoline. This vigorous swing of the arm is enough to create the required half-twist. The idea is to give the performer something to look at on the way down so that the twist is not taken straight from the bed. It is quite easy to tell when the twist comes straight from the bed because the recoil on landing will send the performer towards the side cables. Some coaches using this method have told me that they use 10s. notes as the object to sweep off the bed, telling the performers they can keep the money if they snatch it cleanly! The trouble is that it is an expensive way of getting results.

Having mastered these basic bounces with twists, the really confident performers should be given the task of executing the whole lot in swingtime without any free bounces in between:

half-twist to knees,
half-twist to feet,
half-twist to seat,
half-twist to feet,
half-twist to front,
half-twist to feet,
half-twist to back,
half-twist to feet.

This sequence requires a great deal of thought and control since some of the take-offs are back-to-front, causing a great deal of consternation. It is far more difficult than it looks. Try it!

The next three movements are quite simple but they are intermediate stages in the learning of further twisting movements and, therefore, I will describe them here.

106

Knee Half-twist to Seat. The body, being vertical in the Knee Drop position, makes this movement virtually identical to the half-twist to Seat Drop. As the performer is lifted from the recoil of the bed he should reach forward and upward at an angle of about 30°, twisting the upper half of his body so that this twist will transfer to the rest of his body as he extends. Because of this forward reach, the Seat Drop landing will be an open piked position with the majority of the body weight shared between the seat and hands.

Seat Half-twist to Front. From the Seat Drop, although both hands are in contact with the bed, only one really does any pushing. This one-sided force, together with the head and shoulder turning in the required direction, causes the body to rotate about the longitudinal axis and a landing on the front is performed. If the hands were to push the body upward, the thrust would be from one end of the body only and the landing would be on the knees instead of the front. This incorrect landing is quite usual because a performer is used to pushing with his hands. The head must be kept low since this also will help to keep the body in its correct plane.

Back Half-twist to Front. From the Back Drop landing the legs must be dropped and fully extended so that the body forms a flat horizontal position. The twist is initiated by the lower half of the body turning as the legs are being dropped and extended. It is also possible to assist this twist by pushing one arm across the body whilst still in contact with the bed. Failure to drop the legs could mean an uncomfortable landing for the performer, with the majority of the pressure being on the chest and the legs bending backward causing a hyper-extension in the lumbar region.

Swivel Hips. This is a half-twist to Seat Drop from another Seat Drop. Some people get confused over this movement when writing out routines and finish up with an incorrect number of contacts with the bed. Because this movement can only be performed from a Seat Drop, the initial Seat Drop is quite often included in the terminology of this sequence. There are eight methods by which this combination can be taught. The first is to push harder with one hand when coming up from the initial

107

Seat Drop. This extra force at one side of the body will create a twisting action around the longitudinal axis whilst rotating forward about the lateral axis. The only fault with this method is that because the twist has been initiated from the bed it will remain with the body throughout the movement. Also, because more force was given to one side of the body the whole action will create a sideways cast.

A second method is to swing one arm upward and across the body, turning the shoulders at the same time in the direction of the twist. This action commences from the moment the hands push into the bed to raise the body from the initial Seat Drop. Once again, because the twist is initiated from the bed a casting action is usually perceptible.

The third method is to push from the bed and swing both arms upward and over one shoulder, turning the upper half of the body at the same time. As the performer reaches the vertical position the twisting action is transferred through the rest of the body. The legs are then raised in front of the body for the second Seat Drop. During this movement the legs should be swung fully extended directly under the body, but what usually happens is that the knees are bent up in an effort to accelerate the small amount of forward momentum which is present.

The fourth method is through the lead-up stages of Seat Drop half-twist to feet, Seat half-twist to feet followed by a second Seat Drop and so on. The trouble is that in performing the half-twist early, as in the first stage, the body weight is forward when it must be backward in order to perform the second Seat Drop.

The fifth method is to get the performer to execute a Seat Drop to Front Drop with straight legs. It will be quite noticeable that the legs swing under the body in a straight line whereas in most cases the legs are apt to swing sideways away from the body. Commencing with this action in mind, the arms should reach forward and upward at an angle of about 30°. The shoulders should turn about the longitudinal axis as outlined for the standing half-twist to Seat Drop. We now have a combination for correcting the two most common faults, i.e. the legs swinging round instead of under the body and the body weight moving in the right direction for performing the second Seat

Drop correctly. The sixth method is to call out to the performer a whole sequence of basic drops with half-twists. At some time, when a Seat Drop is being executed, the coach should call, 'Half-twist to Seat'. Because the performer does not have to think too deeply, he will invariably execute the Swivel Hips movement.

By using the manual spotting method the seventh and eighth alternatives can be taught. With the coach standing on the bed to the side of the performer, a Seat Drop is executed with the aid of a *kip* from the coach. As the performer rises from the bed, the coach reaches across to take the performer's farther hand. The twist is then initiated by the coach who pulls the arm towards him, thereby, twisting the upper half of the performer's body. The second Seat Drop landing is made without an intermediate contact with the bed.

Although there are still times when I have to resort to the aforementioned methods, I have found this final method to be the most successful of all. The preliminary stages are exactly the same as for the last method. The coach stands on the bed beside the performer and assists by *kipping* the first Seat Drop landing. As the performer rises to the vertical position, the coach reaches across with one hand and rotates the performer's hips. The hand follows through under the legs lifting them in preparation for the final landing. So long as the finished product is exactly what is required, it does not matter which method is used.

Roller. A full twist to Seat Drop from another Seat Drop. Again, the initial Seat Drop is usually included in the terminology for this movement. Invariably a coach can get away with demonstrating this movement and then telling his students to try it. However, for the difficult student, the first stage is to perform consecutive Seat Drops with the hips being raised forward and the feet being forced downward whilst in the air, so that the body is in a straight line. The bouncer needs to feel this position because it must be in this position that the full twist is performed. On take-off from the Seat Drop, one hand pushes harder into the bed, causing the shoulders to rotate around the longitudinal axis. This rotation is accelerated by the hips being

109

snapped round in the same direction as they are lifted to the straight position. When the full rotation is completed the body can bend at the hips again for the second Seat Drop. If this second Seat Drop position is premature, the twist will be slowed down and the performer will finish up sitting across the bed instead of being along its length. Emphasis should be on pushing the body round the longitudinal axis rather than upward. If forward rotation is present, the performer will only complete a half-twist and finish on his knees. It was for this reason that the Seat half-twist to Front Drop movement was described. It may mean that this should be performed as an intermediate stage. Another aid in executing this movement is for the performer to bounce at one end of the trampoline with his feet hanging over the suspension system. The coach grasps hold of the ankles and bounces the performer into three consecutive Seat Drops and then assists in rotating him by turning his feet in the required direction. The final correction, which is sometimes required, is to tell the performer to throw his hips in the opposite direction to the rotation (same as for somersaults), thereby eliminating any cast.

Cradle. This movement is a half-twist to Back Drop from another Back Drop. The lead-up stage is to perform a Back Drop to Front Drop in a hollow-back position. This can be achieved by swinging the legs away and downward vigorously and at the same time lifting the hips for a good hip extension. This action only should be used. There must be no effort to raise the shoulders from the bed. When the performer can see the bed, and not before, the half-twist should be created as described earlier for the half-twist to Back Drop movement.

Corkscrew. This is a one and a half twist to Back Drop from another Back Drop. The basic requirements for performing this movement are exactly the same as for the cradle. The only difference is that with a Corkscrew one and a half twists are performed between each Back Drop whereas for the Cradle only a half-twist is executed. In order to give the performer confidence that this movement is possible, and above all that he can do it, the twisting action should be practised. From a standing position, first a half-twist to Back Drop should be performed, then a full twist to Front Drop and, finally, one and a half twists to Back Drop. The performer can then prove to himself that the full twisting action can be completed in the second half of the movement. Now, to get the feeling of the take-off, a Back Drop with half-twist to feet and a Back Drop full twist to feet should be executed. Knowing how to initiate the twist on take-off, and also that a one and a half twist can be completed within the time allocated, the performer is ready to try for the full movement.

Cat-twist. This movement is a full twist to Back Drop from another Back Drop. It gets its name from the action a cat makes to land on its feet properly, if falling upside-down. There are various ways in which the twist can be initiated. One is by using the hips to rotate the body about the longitudinal axis on take-off. This looks like the actual cat's twist action where one half of the body moves round a half a turn followed by the other half of the body. This is repeated until the full twist is completed. Another method is for one arm to be pushed across the chest as the performer recoils from the bed on the first Back Drop. By continually pushing this arm and straightening the body at the same time, the twist is transferred to the rest of the body. The third method is to push the hand of the twisting arm into the bed on take-off. This push into the bed will force that shoulder to move across the chest and, therefore, create the twist from the shoulders. Another method is to bang the elbow of the twisting arm into the bed as the body rises. This late contact with the bed creates a Kaboom action which in turn throws this arm across the chest, initiating the required twist. The first lead-up stage is to perform what is known as a *Vertical Arch*. This is where, following a Back Drop, the body is fully extended in an inverted position with the eyes looking at the bed. The head is then tucked under once more and the performer returns to the Back Drop position. To most people this is a more difficult movement than the Cat-twist itself. Having the face so close to the bed whilst the rest of the body is vertical is quite an alarming experience. From the Back Drop, the legs should be pushed over the performer's face, at the same time as the body is fully extended and the head is dropped back to look at the bed. The difficulty here is making

111

certain that the legs remain in this perpendicular position whilst the performer is looking at the bed. So often the legs drop and the correct body position cannot be maintained. The performer must realize that as soon as the top half of the body and the head are pulled back to look for the bed, there will be an equal reaction from the legs at the other end of the body. It is this reaction which causes the legs to drop. The remedy, therefore, is for the legs to be pushed farther over the face than is thought necessary on take-off. The reaction will then bring them back over the centre of the body to the correct position. Having mastered this action, the full movement can then be executed by using one of the methods of twisting mentioned earlier. It is possible to carry out some resemblance to this Cat-twist with the body almost in a horizontal position. The performers with the more timid approach may even build up from this position rather than try to master the vertical arch. In this case, an intermediate stage may be the Back Drop, half-twist to Front Drop, which was described earlier. Gradually, the legs should be raised until a more acceptable position is achieved and the full twist movement completed.

I have found the easiest and most successful method of teaching this movement has been from a combination of this last idea together with manual spotting. The coach stands to the side of the performer and initiates the twist by pulling the performer's farther arm across the body and turning him on to his back. The performer only has to think about a good Back Drop, the coach guides the twisting action and places the performer into a good landing position.

43. Coleen Melvin and Marijke van den Boogard presenting Ted Blake with a souvenir from Africa during the World Championships 1965.

44. A full twisting back somersault performed by Nancy Smith, U.S.A. at the Second World Championships 1965.

45. Gary Erwin and Frank Schmitz winning the World Synchronized Championships, 1965.

46. Gary Erwin, U.S.A., performing a Rudolph during the 1965 World Championships at the Royal Albert Hall.

47. The first three place winners congratulate each other on the rostrum during the World Championships 1965.

48. Lynda Ball and Barbara John of England watch in amazement one of the performers in the Second World Championships 1965.

8

Twisting Somersaults and Fliffes

There are many different teaching methods for all these movements. I am just putting forward those with which I have achieved the most success.

Barani. This is a forward somersault with half-twist. The Barani was named after Joe Barani, an acrobat who performed this movement on the ground way back in the 1890's.

There are really two main methods of teaching this movement; one from the knees and one from the feet. The idea of the first method from the knees is to bring the centre of gravity of the performer low to the bed so that there is a greater margin for error.

(a) Get the performer to execute a Knee Drop to handstand.

(b) Repeat (a), looking at the bed all the time, and fall over to a flat back landing.

(c) As the performer falls backward, having passed the vertical, he should push on one hand to create a half-twist to Front Drop or Hands-and-Knees Drop.

(d) On take-off, the knees should dig hard into the bed in order to stretch the suspension system as much as possible. The resultant stronger recoil should force the performer higher, enabling him to repeat (c) but to land on his feet.

(e) Once again the knees should be pushed into the bed on take-off and the hips lifted so high that the hands cannot touch the bed during the movement. As the body moves to the vertical, the legs should be swung upward and twisted at the same time. As the body is straightened, the twist is

H   113

transferred to the rest of the body. The important thing is that the twist is not put on too early. When this stage is mastered, the whole movement can be taken from the feet.

The second method relies upon the performer being able to execute a good forward somersault in the piked or half-lever position first. Since a Barani is a forward somersault with half-twist, all that is required is the half-twist.

(a) Get the performer to show a good somersault in the half-lever position.

(b) To give an indication as to the likely direction he may twist, a half-twist to Back Drop may help. This doesn't always work but it is something on which to base your reasoning.

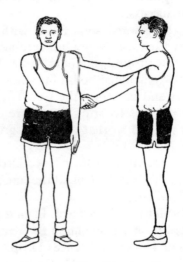

Fig. 21

(c) The coach should now stand on the bed with the performer. The performer's twisting arm should be placed across his body to hold the hand of the coach, who is facing the performer's side. The performer's loose arm should hang in front of his body across the coach's arm, which is holding the twisting arm (Fig. 21). The loose arm is placed in this position in order to keep the shoulders

114

square to the line along which the stunt will be performed.

(d) The performer should execute an open forward somersault, maintaining this grip so that he can familiarize himself with this unnatural position.

(e) Repeat (d), but this time the coach should pull on the performer's twisting arm and push on his opposite shoulder. This action will create the twist and should be initiated when the upper half of the performer's body is vertical to the bed.

(f) The performer should look at the centre of the bed throughout this movement. As he begins to orientate himself he should be encouraged to think about the timing of the twisting action. After a few Baranis with the coach creating the twist, the performer should call out at the moment he thinks the twist should begin. If, and when, this coincides with the timing by the coach, the performer should push his twisting arm across his body with the coach still guiding and controlling the movement.

(g) The coach should now let the performer gradually take over the whole movement.

Rudolph. Forward somersault with one and a half twists. It is said that the first man to perform this movement was Sig Meely, a comic in a professional act, way back in 1901 or 1902. He called the movement a Rudolph but no one knows why.

(a) Knee Drop, at one end of the bed, with a hollow-back forward-turnover to a flat-back landing. To assist this movement the head must be pressed well back throughout until the landing. The emphasis should be on the heel lift rather than hips.

(b) As the hips and heels lift the performer from the bed, an arm should be pushed across the chest. This arm should continue to push until the body has passed through 360° so that once again a flat-back landing can be made. Since the head is pressed well back, the performer should look for the bed all the way round.

(c) From a Knee Drop take-off, the body should be projected high from the bed so that a full twisting somersault to feet can be executed. Again, the performer should watch the bed throughout so that on landing he is looking over one shoulder.

(d) At this point the coach must use his discretion in the knowledge of his pupil. Some performers are not as happy as others about Front Drop landings.

Either: From a Knee Drop take-off, continue to push the twisting arm across the chest until one and a half twists are executed and a landing is made in a Front Drop position or on hands and knees.

Or: From the Knee Drop take-off, push out of the bed for height and perform a one and a half twisting front somersault to feet. The difference between this and (c) above is that the twisting arm is pushed harder, and for longer across the chest.

(e) When the performer knows where he is and what he is doing from the knees, he can then take the full movement from his feet. The somersault action must be created first with the twisting action coming just before the upper half of the body reaches the vertical. As the twist is initiated, the legs should be snapped upward, bringing the body in line.

Randolph. Forward somersault with two and a half twists. When the performer is ready for this movement he will have executed the Rudolph so often that it will purely be a case of more power on take-off, twisting slightly earlier and holding on.

Full Twisting Back Somersault. This has now been shortened and is known universally as a *Back with Full.* The two methods by which I have found the most success with this movement are:

(a) Three-quarter back somersault to Front Drop.

(b) Repeat (a) but as the performer sees the bed he should swing one arm across the body to perform a Lazy Back with half-twist to a flat Back Drop.

(c) The above should now be executed from the feet round to feet again into a half-twisting layout back somersault. The cue for initiating the twist should be the sighting of the bed. By performing it in this manner when learning, the student knows where he is before initiating rotation about a second axis.

(d) Similarly as with the Rudolph, we arrive at the point

116

where the coach must make a decision regarding Front Drop landings for his student.

Either: A full twisting Lazy back can be executed before going from feet to feet.

Or: The performer can go straight from feet to feet, edging round in the twist as he feels confident.

The second method is based on the mechanics of shortening the Moment of Inertia on one side of the body. This method is really quite straightforward:

(a) Get the performer to execute a layout back somersault with both arms raised above his head all the way round.

(b) Tell the performer to throw one arm down to his side at a point when his feet are above his head. The other arm must be kept raised above his head. The arm thrown down to the side will cause a shortening of the Moment of Inertia on that side so that the body will rotate in this direction.

(c) All that will be required after this are general coaching points, as applicable, to get the performer to land in an upright position on the completion of the movement.

Double Twisting Back Somersault; Triple Twisting Back Somersault. Each of these is a natural development on its predecessor and only requires more force on take-off and a slightly earlier twist.

From the single somersaults with twists we progress to the double somersaults with twists; these are known as *Fliffes*. It is said that the word fliffis originated from the flip-twist. There is no limit as to the number of twists performed but a double somersault must be executed each time. The twist may occur in the first somersault; the second somersault; mid-way between the two or even during both somersaults. The order in which I am going to write about these is for convenience and not necessarily the chronological order of learning. Although I am not going to mention specifically when a twisting belt and rig should be used, I am going to list the progressions which should be followed either with or without the rig. The coach must use his discretion for which performers and at which point this apparatus is required.

Half-out Fliffis. The performer must be able to execute a forward one and three-quarter somersault and a Barani before attempting this movement.

(a) Perform a one and three-quarter forward somersault so that the way out can be seen clearly and a crash-dive landing on to the back can be made.

(b) Increase the early rotation of the one and three-quarter somersault so that the opening to a crash dive can be made with as much height from the bed as possible.

(c) Next, get the performer to execute a standing Barani movement to hands and knees. The reason for landing on hands and knees is because it is safe.

(d) Repeat (c), delaying the twisting action for as long as possible so that a position near to a crash dive is possible before creating the twist.

(e) Perform a one and three-quarter somersault, coming out early and looking at the bed for the landing. The performer should think of creating the twist whilst in the crash dive position.

(f) When confidence has been gained over the correct timing of the twist, one or two standing Baranis should be performed, again in order to refresh the memory as to the feeling.

(g) On the completion of the one and three-quarter forward somersault, the legs should be allowed to travel over the head before creating the twist. The landing for the first one or two attempts should be to hands and knees for safety.

A useful movement which may also be used as a progression for the Half-out fliffis is a Ball-out Barani.

(a) From a Back Drop the performer should turn over in an open tucked position to point to the bed momentarily and then tuck under at the last minute to land on his back. This pointing to the bed enables the performer to orientate himself and see exactly at which point the twist should be created.

(b) By pointing at the bed the arm is extended in front of the body. This arm only has to be pushed across the chest for

118

the twist to be initiated. The landing to begin with can be made on to the hands and knees until the confidence is such that more rotation can be initiated on take-off.

Rudy-out Fliffis. This is where the Rudolph, or one and a half twisting forward somersault is performed during the second somersault. The progressions for this movement are very similar to those for the Half-out fliffis. For obvious reasons the performer must have mastered the Rudolph and the Half-out fliffis before attempting this movement. It is with this movement in particular that the one and a half twisting Ball-out is a most useful progression.

Barani-in Fliffis. This is a forward movement where the half-twist is performed during the first somersault.

(a) Get the performer to execute an early twist Cradle.

(b) Increase the rotation by starting with more height and swinging the legs on take-off from the back. It is also possible to build up momentum by performing a one and three-quarter somersault. With this increased rotation, take the early twisted Cradle right over to feet so that in actual fact a Back Drop followed by a half-twist into a back somersault is performed. This is the baby-fliffis which is used more than any other.

(c) Perform an overthrown Barani into a Back Pull-over.

(d) Go for the full movement. The take-off must be forceful with maximum forward rotation. Wait, before creating the twist. Although this movement is known as an early twist fliffis, the twist must not be too early.

Back-in, Full-out Fliffis. This is a double backward somersault with a full-twist in the second somersault.

(a) Perform double backward somersaults gradually opening out during the second somersault. As the tucked position is opened, the performer will be able to see more of where he is during this second somersault.

(b) One and a quarter somersault with a late half-twist to Front Drop.

(c) When the one and a quarter back with half-twist is performed easily with control, increase the height and rota-

119

tion on take-off so that instead of landing in a Front Drop position this can be changed to a crash dive, tucking the head under at the last minute.

(d) Some may now like to increase the rotation even further and perform a one and three-quarter somersault to a flat back landing.

(e) Repeat (d), creating the twist at the same point in the rotation but increasing the twist to a full 360° to a Front Drop.

(f) Increase rotation further making the landing on to hands and knees. Some performers may like to jump straight to this stage from (c), making the movement a double back somersault to hands and knees with a full-twist in the second somie.

(g) By increasing the rotation further still, the full movement feet-to-feet can be achieved.

Full-in, Back-out. This is a double backward somersault with a full-twist in the first somersault.

(a) The performer must first be able to execute a controlled, full twisting backward somersault and a flying double backward somersault. The flying double backward somersault is where the first somersault is performed in a layout position and the second somersault tucked.

(b) Get the performer to execute an overthrown full twisting backward somersault to Back Drop.

(c) Repeat (b) followed by a Back Pull-over.

(d) The full movement must now be executed. The rotation of the first somersault must be fast and vigorous with the twist coming late in this somersault. The tucking for the second somersault will accelerate the latter half of the movement.

Half-in, Half-out Fliffis. Another backward double somersault this time with a half-twist in the first somersault and a half-twist in the second somersault. The complete movement at the moment is being performed in what is known as the *pucked* position. This is where the body attains an open tucked attitude throughout the stunt. I believe that in time we shall see this type of movement performed in the layout position.

(a) The bouncer should first perform a layout backward

somersault with half-twist. The twist should not be initiated until the bed is sighted so that the rotation is well and truly underway and the performer can orientate himself during the movement.

(b) Repeat (a) gradually drawing up the knees until the movement can be performed in the open tucked position.

(c) Increase the rotation so that an overthrown back somersault with half-twist to Front Drop is executed. Remember that it is important to initiate the twist only after the bed has been sighted. This will mean that the bed is seen twice; once during the twist and once as the Front Drop is made.

(d) When the performer really knows where he is and can see the bed properly each time, increase the amount of rotation once more so that the head can be tucked under and a landing made on to the back. The movement now being performed is an overthrown back somersault with half-twist into a crash dive.

(e) To complete the movement, the last part is the same as for the Half-out fliffis. Therefore, the performer could repeat the stunt just to get the feeling of the final half-twist from a forward somersaulting movement whilst looking at the bed. The direction of the second half-twist should be the same as for the first. Coaches should check that their performers do, in actual fact, execute the backward somersault with half-twist in the same direction as a normal Barani. If this is not the case then one or other of the movements should be relearned.

(f) The full movement can now be performed with, perhaps, the first one or two landing on hands and knees.

Half-in, Full-out Fliffis. This is a forward double somersault with a half-twist in the first somersault and a full twist in the second somersault.

(a) Since the beginning of this movement is the same as for the Barani-in fliffis, it is obvious that this movement should be mastered first. Likewise, the final part of the fliffis is the same as for the Back-in full-out fliffis and, again, should be mastered before coupling the two together.

(b) First, overthrow the Barani to a Back Drop landing.

(c) Perform a one and three-quarter somersault with an early half-twist. Once the Barani has been performed the remainder will be as for a one and three-quarter backward somersault to Front Drop.

(d) The idea behind executing the last movement is that the performer can see the bed during the second somersault and be aware of his position in the air. When he can do this safely, he is then ready to try for the full movement. Again, the first few attempts may be to hands and knees.

Full-in, Full-out Fliffis. A backward double somersault with a full twist in each somersault.

(a) Practise performing a low full twisting backward somersault in the open tucked position. By performing this somersault without much height the emphasis must be placed on a powerful take-off and the speed of rotation.

(b) Overturn this full twisting backward somersault to a Back Drop.

(c) Repeat (b) but include an extra half-twist so that a one and a half twisting one and a quarter backward somersault to front drop is performed.

(d) Increase the rotation on (c) so that the last part of the movement can be turned into a crash dive to Back Drop.

(e) The performer should continue to practise the above movement until he is completely aware of his position as he performs the crash dive at the end of (d). The overall height and rotation should then be increased and a Barani executed as the performer comes out of the movement for the crash dive. The full movement is then completed.

Because there are so many combinations as to the method in which the twists can be applied in fliffis movements there are too many to list them all here. I have selected the most popular ones which are used for the half; full; one and a half; and double twists.

9

Swingtime Routines

When starting competition work so many performers and their coaches seem to have great difficulty in compiling suitable routines. Either the combinations selected do not flow smoothly one into the other or an incorrect number of movements is performed. To help these people over their problem I shall explain what I feel to be the best methods of procedure.

The first thing to do is to list the competitor's best stunts, either because of their difficulty rating or because of the assurance of their execution. Let us suppose that the following movements, therefore, are the ones we would like to consider for the next competition:

Rudolph.
Cody.
Layout back somersault.
Full twisting back.
Three-quarter Lazy Back somersault.
Cradle.
Barani.
Turntable.

There are four main factors which help to determine the order of the movements performed:

Difficulty. Stunts which require maximum height and an extra steady take-off.

Body Momentum. Movements are easier and flow more smoothly when performed in the direction of the body momentum already set up during the routine.

Landing/Take-off Position. A movement where the take-off is other than from the feet requires the appropriate corresponding landing before this movement can be executed, e.g.— Cody. If a Cody is to be performed, then it is no use writing down a Rudolph as the preceding stunt. A movement must be selected which finishes with a Front Drop landing, e.g. three-quarter Lazy Back somersault. (This may seem obvious to most of you but this type of thing actually happens on far too many occasions.) People list 8 or 10 individual stunts without thinking of landings, take-offs or combinations.

Position on the Bed. Imagine a performer who throws a Ball-out movement way down the length of the bed. His sequence of movements is:

> One and three-quarter forward somersault;
> Ball-out to feet;
> Barani.

By the time he reaches this stage it may be provoking providence to add a backward movement to the end of this sequence. Therefore, a stunt should be selected which would return the performer to the centre of the bed.

With this knowledge we can then continue. Number down the page 1–8 so that the name of each movement can be placed in chronological order beside its corresponding number. In this way the movements can be read at a glance and there is a constant reminder as to the number of movements still required at any given time.

Bearing in mind that most performers gradually lose height during a swingtime routine we must think of beginning with the most difficult movements. In this way we can be sure that sufficient height is available and the performer is perfectly balanced before take-off. From the list, therefore, I would select the Rudolph.

The body momentum is now in a backward direction and, therefore, anything backward would flow smoothly from this. From our lists we have three choices: Layout backward somersault; full twisting back; and three-quarter Lazy back somie. The latter movement has a Front Drop landing which would normally diminish any height previously obtained, therefore, we do not want to use that one at this stage. The remaining two are

124

both layout backward somersaults but one has a full twist in it. There are two considerations here.

(a) A complicated movement has just been performed, should a steadying movement follow?

(b) Should a performer begin with his two big tricks together leaving little in the judges' minds when they come to give their scores?

Taking these points to thought I would place the layout backward somersault as my second movement. As with all landings from a backward rotation the performer is able to come out of the rotation early to land short and thereby keeping his body weight in front of the point of landing. The natural direction on take-off again would be with forward rotation. This would lead nicely into the Barani which changes direction to give backward momentum into the full twisting backward movement.

Looking at the stunts left which we would like to include, we have to think carefully. There are four more bounces left to gain as many points as possible. From feet back to feet again the turntable would take three of the four bounces and would give a difficulty rating of ·4 points. The Cradle would also require three bounces in order to return to feet and give a difficulty rating of only ·5. On the other hand the Lazy Back somersault into a Cody back to feet would give a difficulty rating of ·8 and still leave two further bounces to increase the total tariff value. We must, therefore, give preference to the latter combination and exclude the other two. Continuing with the original list of selected movements I would repeat the Barani in the straight position as the fifth stunt followed by the three-quarter Lazy back somie and Cody as numbers six and seven and then finish with a backward somersault. The body momentum after the Barani is backward and the three remaining movements are in this direction, they should, therefore, swing quite smoothly one into the other. The complete routine would then be:

1. Rudolph.	6. ¾ Lazy back somie.
2. Layout back somie.	7. Cody.
3. Barani. (B).	8. Back somie. (C).
4. Full twisting backward somie.	Out bounce.
5. Barani. (A).	

To assist you in selecting routines for competitions and for the general training of your squad, here are a number of 8-bounce and 10-bounce routines.

8-Bounce Routines

1. Tuck Jump.
2. Back Drop.
3. ½-twist to feet.
4. Piked Straddle.
5. ½-twist to Front Drop.
6. To feet.
7. ½-twist to seat.
8. ½-twist to feet.

1. Tuck Jump.
2. Splits Jump.
3. Back somersault.
4. Seat Drop.
5. Swivel Hips.
6. Knee bounce.
7. ¾ forward turnover to back.
8. To feet.

1. Splits Jump.
2. Vertical ½-twist jump.
3. Piked straddle.
4. Full pirouette.
5. Tuck Jump.
6. Back somersault.
7. Piked Jump.
8. Forward somersault.

1. Splits Jump.
2. Full pirouette.
3. Piked Straddle Jump.
4. Back somersault.
5. Seat Drop.
6. Swivel Hips.
7. Roller.
8. ½-twist to feet.

1. Full pirouette.
2. Tuck Jump.
3. Back Drop.
4. ½-twist to feet.
5. Seat Drop.
6. Swivel Hips.
7. To feet.
8. Forward somersault (c).

1. Piked Straddle Jump.
2. Back somersault.
3. Splits Jump.
4. ½-twist to seat.
5. ½-twist to feet.
6. Full pirouette.
7. Piked Straddle Jump.
8. Back somersault.

1. Splits Jump.
2. Full pirouette.
3. Seat Drop.
4. Swivel Hips.
5. ½-twist to feet.
6. Knee Drop.
7. Forward turnover to back.
8. ½-twist to feet.

1. Back somersault.
2. Tuck Jump.
3. Splits Jump.
4. Full pirouette.
5. Seat Drop.
6. Swivel Hips.
7. Knee Drop.
8. Forward somersault.

126

1. Tuck Jump.
2. Piked Straddle Jump.
3. Back somersault.
4. Seat Drop.
5. Swivel Hips.
6. Roller.
7. Knee Drop.
8. Forward somersault.

1. Full pirouette.
2. Seat Drop.
3. Swivel Hips.
4. ½-twist to knees.
5. ½-twist to feet.
6. Straddle Jump.
7. Forward somersault to Seat Drop.
8. ½-twist to feet.

1. Full-twist to Back Drop.
2. Cradle.
3. ½-twist to feet.
4. ½-twist vertical jump.
5. Pike Straddle Jump.
6. Full pirouette.
7. Forward somersault to seat.
8. ½-twist to feet.

1. Full pirouette.
2. Piked Straddle Jump.
3. Back somersault.
4. Seat Drop.
5. Swivel Hips.
6. ½-twist to feet.
7. Tuck Jump.
8. Forward somersault.

1. Piked Straddle Jump.
2. Full pirouette.
3. Piked Jump.
4. Back somersault.
5. Full-twist to Back Drop.
6. ½-twist to feet.
7. Tuck Jump.
8. Forward somersault.

1. Back somersault.
2. Splits Jump.
3. Full pirouette.
4. Seat Drop.
5. Swivel Hips.
6. ½-twist to feet.
7. Piked Straddle Jump.
8. Forward somersault.

1. Splits Jump.
2. ½-twist vertical jump.
3. Piked Straddle Jump.
4. Full pirouette.
5. Back somersault.
6. Piked Straddle Jump.
7. Barani.
8. Forward somersault.

1. Back somersault.
2. Splits Jump.
3. Back somersault.
4. ½-twist to seat.
5. ½-twist to feet.
6. Piked Straddle Jump.
7. Knee bounce.
8. Forward somersault.

1. Back somersault.
2. Piked Straddle Jump.
3. Tuck Jump.
4. Back somersault to seat.
5. Swivel Hips.
6. ½-twist to feet.
7. Piked Straddle Jump.
8. Full pirouette.

1. Back somersault.
2. Piked Straddle Jump.
3. Seat Drop.
4. Swivel Hips.
5. ½-twist to knees.
6. Forward somie to seat.
7. ½-twist to feet.
8. Full pirouette.

1. Back somersault to seat.
2. Swivel Hips.
3. ½-twist to feet.
4. Piked Straddle Jump.
5. Forward somersault.
6. Front Drop.
7. Back turnover to Back Drop.
8. ½-twist to feet.

1. Full pirouette.
2. Back somersault.
3. Barani.
4. ½-twist to Front Drop.
5. Back Drop.
6. ½-twist to feet.
7. Piked Jump.
8. Forward somersault.

1. Back somersault.
2. Splits Jump.
3. Back somersault.
4. ½-twist to seat.
5. ½-twist to feet.
6. Piked Straddle Jump.
7. Knee bounce.
8. Forward somersault.

1. Piked Straddle Jump.
2. Back somersault.
3. Seat Drop.
4. Swivel Hips.
5. ½-twist to feet.
6. Barani.
7. Back somersault.
8. Forward somersault.

1. Piked Straddle Jump.
2. Full pirouette.
3. Piked Jump.
4. Back somersault.
5. Full-twist to Back Drop.
6. ½-twist to feet.
7. Tuck Jump.
8. Forward somersault.

1. Back somersault.
2. Piked Straddle Jump.
3. Barani.
4. Back Drop.
5. Cradle.
6. ½-twist to feet.
7. Back 1¼ somersault.
8. ½-twist to feet.

1. ½-twist vertical jump.
2. Barani.
3. Piked Straddle Jump.
4. Back somersault.
5. ½-twist to Back Drop.
6. Cradle.
7. ½-twist to feet.
8. Full pirouette.

1. Back somersault.
2. Piked Straddle Jump.
3. Barani.
4. Full pirouette.
5. Forward somersault.
6. ½-twist to Back Drop.
7. Cradle.
8. Full-twist to feet.

1. Lazy back somersault
2. Back turnover to Back Drop.
3. ½–twist to feet.
4. Tuck Jump.
5. Barani.
6. Back somersault.
7. Piked Straddle Jump.
8. Forward somersault.

1. Back somersault.
2. Barani.
3. Back Drop.
4. Cradle.
5. ½-twist to feet.
6. Tuck Jump.
7. Back 1¼ somersault.
8. ½-twist to feet.

49. (*Above*) The trophy winners line up after the finals of the Second World Championships 1965.

50. The author, Beverley Averyt and American team coach Jeff Hennessy exchange ideas during the World Championships.

51. The British and American teams line up to be presented to the Wembley audience. The trampolinists are, *from the right:* Mike Williams (5th), Lynda Ball (8th), Beverley Averyt (13th) and Keen Day (20th).

52. (*Left*) Judy Wills, World Trampolining and Tumbling Champion 1964, 1965, 1966, 1967, shows that many of the trampolining movements can be performed on the ground in a tumbling sequence.

55. (*Above*) Dave Curtis performing a Barani showing the assymetric line of the arms with the body.

56. (*Below*) The German Synchronized Trampolining team.

53. The victory ceremony following the Ladies' Competition.

54. The finest trampolinists in the World on the victory rostrum.

1. Back somersault.
2. Barani.
3. Piked Straddle Jump.
4. Full pirouette.
5. Forward somersault.
6. ½-twist vertical jump.
7. Back 1¼ somersault.
8. ½-twist to feet.

1. Back somersault.
2. Barani.
3. Back Drop.
4. Cradle.
5. ½-twist to feet.
6. Tuck Jump.
7. Back 1¼ somersault.
8. ½-twist to feet.

1. Full pirouette.
2. Crash dive.
3. Ball-out to feet.
4. ½-twist to Back Drop.
5. ½-twist to feet.
6. Back somersault.
7. Lazy back somersault.
8. Back Cody.

1. Back somersault.
2. Piked Straddle Jump.
3. Barani.
4. Back somersault.
5. Forward somersault.
6. Full-twist to Back Drop.
7. Cradle.
8. ½-twist to feet.

1. Back somersault.
2. Back somersault.
3. Barani.
4. Forward somersault.
5. Full-twist to Back Drop.
6. Cradle.
7. Cat-twist.
8. ½-twist to feet.

1. Lazy back somersault.
2. Back Cody.
3. Piked Straddle Jump.
4. Back somersault.
5. Barani.
6. Crash dive.
7. ½-twist to feet.
8. Forward somersault.

1. Back somersault.
2. Barani.
3. Back somersault.
4. Full pirouette.
5. Barani.
6. Piked Straddle Jump.
7. Piked ¾ back somersault.
8. Cody.

1. Back somersault.
2. Splits Jump.
3. Back somersault.
4. Barani.
5. Full pirouette.
6. Lazy back somersault.
7. Cody.
8. Forward somersault.

1. Back somersault.
2. Piked Straddle Jump.
3. Back somersault to seat.
4. Swivel Hips.
5. ½-twist to feet.
6. Back somersault.
7. Barani.
8. Back somersault.

1. Back somersault.
2. Full pirouette.
3. Barani.
4. Back 1¼ somersault.
5. Cradle.
6. ½-twist to feet.
7. Back somersault.
8. Barani.

1. Back somersault.
2. Barani.
3. Tuck back somersault.
4. Full-twist to Back Drop.
5. To feet.
6. Piked Straddle Jump.
7. $1\frac{3}{4}$ forward somersault.
8. Ball-out to feet.

1. Back somersault.
2. Barani.
3. Back somie to seat.
4. Swivel Hips.
5. $\frac{1}{2}$-twist to feet.
6. Full pirouette.
7. Lazy back somersault.
8. Back Cody.

1. Rudolph.
2. Piked Straddle Jump.
3. Back somersault.
4. Barani.
5. Back somersault.
6. Piked Straddle Jump.
7. Piked $\frac{3}{4}$ back somersault.
8. Back Cody.

1. Back somersault.
2. Barani.
3. Back somersault.
4. Forward somersault.
5. Barani.
6. $\frac{1}{2}$-twist to Back Drop.
7. Cradle.
8. Full-twist to feet.

1. Back somersault.
2. $\frac{1}{2}$-twist to Front Drop.
3. $\frac{1}{2}$-twist to feet.
4. Back somersault.
5. Barani.
6. Back somersault.
7. Crash dive.
8. Ball-out to feet.

1. Back somersault.
2. Barani.
3. Back somersault.
4. Full-twist to Back Drop.
5. Half-twist to feet.
6. Piked Straddle Jump.
7. $1\frac{3}{4}$ front somersault.
8. Ball-out to feet.

1. Back somersault.
2. Barani.
3. Back with full-twist.
4. Barani.
5. Back somersault.
6. Lazy back somersault.
7. Cody.
8. Forward somersault.

1. Back somersault.
2. Barani.
3. Back somersault.
4. Full pirouette.
5. Barani.
6. Back with full-twist.
7. Back somersault.
8. Back with full-twist.

1. $1\frac{3}{4}$ forward somersault.
2. Ball-out Barani.
3. Piked Straddle Jump.
4. Back with full-twist.
5. Barani.
6. Back somersault.
7. Back somersault.
8. Rudolph.

1. Back with full-twist.
2. Barani.
3. Back somersault.
4. Lazy back somersault.
5. Back Cody.
6. Back somersault.
7. Crash dive.
8. Ball-out to feet.

1. Back somersault.
2. Back somie with ½-twist.
3. Barani.
4. Back with full-twist.
5. Barani.
6. Rudolph.
7. Back 1¼ somersault.
8. Full-twist to feet.

1. Rudolph.
2. Piked Straddle Jump.
3. Barani.
4. Back with full-twist.
5. Barani.
6. Back somersault.
7. 1¾ forward somersault.
8. Barani Ball-out.

10-Bounce Routines

1. Lazy back somersault.
2. ½-twist to feet.
3. Tuck Jump.
4. Seat Drop.
5. Swivel Hips.
6. ½-twist to feet.
7. Piked Jump.
8. Barani.
9. Piked Straddle Jump.
10. Back somersault.

1. Back somersault.
2. Barani.
3. Splits Jump.
4. Back with full-twist.
5. Full pirouette.
6. Back somersault.
7. Barani.
8. Piked Straddle Jump.
9. Lazy back.
10. Cody.

1. 1½ twisting vertical jump.
2. Tuck Jump.
3. Crash dive.
4. ½-twist to feet.
5. ½-twist to Back Drop.
6. ½-twist to feet.
7. Back somersault.
8. Barani.
9. Piked Straddle Jump.
10. Back somersault.

1. 1¾ forward somersault.
2. ½-twist to feet.
3. Back somersault.
4. Barani.
5. Lazy back somersault.
6. Back Cody.
7. Piked Straddle Jump.
8. Barani.
9. Back somersault.
10. Back with full-twist.

1. Lazy back somersault.
2. Back Cody.
3. Piked Straddle Jump.
4. Back somersault.
5. Barani.
6. Crash dive.
7. ½-twist to feet.
8. Full pirouette.
9. Back somersault.
10. Forward somersault.

1. 1¼ back somersault.
2. Cradle.
3. Back pullover to feet.
4. Back somersault.
5. Rudolph.
6. Back somersault.
7. Back with full-twist.
8. Barani.
9. Lazy back somersault.
10. Back Cody.

1. Lazy back somersault.
2. Back Cody.
3. Back somersault.
4. Rudolph.
5. Crash dive.
6. ½-twist to feet.
7. Back somersault.
8. Rudolph.
9. Barani.
10. Back with full-twist.

---

1. 1¾ forward somersault.
2. Barani Ball-out.
3. Back somersault.
4. Back with full-twist.
5. Barani.
6. Back somersault.
7. Lazy back somersault.
8. Back Cody.
9. Back somersault.
10. Forward somersault.

---

1. Back with full-twist.
2. Back somersault.
3. Barani.
4. Back somersault.
5. Lazy back somersault.
6. Back Cody.
7. Back somersault.
8. Barani.
9. Back with full-twist.
10. Rudolph.

---

1. Back with full-twist.
2. Back somersault.
3. Crash dive.
4. Ball-out Barani.
5. Back somersault.
6. Lazy back somersault.
7. Back Cody.
8. Rudolph.
9. Back somersault.
10. Double backward somersault.

---

1. Double back somersault.
2. Over-thrown Barani to Back Drop.
3. Back Pull-over to feet.
4. Back somersault.
5. Rudolph.
6. Back somersault.
7. Back with full-twist.
8. Barani.
9. Lazy back somersault.
10. Back Cody to feet.

---

1. 1¾ forward somersault.
2. Ball-out Barani.
3. Back somersault.
4. Rudolph.
5. Back somersault.
6. Barani.
7. Back with full-twist.
8. Barani.
9. Lazy back somersault.
10. Cody.

---

1. Double back somersault.
2. Barani.
3. Back with full-twist.
4. Back somersault.
5. Back with double-twist.
6. Back somersault.
7. Piked Straddle Jump.
8. Back somersault.
9. 1¾ back somersault.
10. Back Cody.

---

1. Double back somersault.
2. Back somersault.
3. Back with full-twist.
4. Back somersault.
5. Barani.
6. Lazy back somersault.
7. Back Cody.
8. Back somersault.
9. Double back somersault.
10. Back with double-twist.

1. Full-in back-out fliffis.
2. Barani.
3. Back somersault.
4. Rudolph.
5. Back somersault.
6. Lazy back somersault.
7. Back Cody.
8. Barani.
9. Back with full-twist.
10. Rudolph.

1. Double back somersault.
2. $1\frac{3}{4}$ forward somersault.
3. Barani Ball-out.
4. Back with full-twist.
5. Back with full-twist.
6. Back with full-twist.
7. Barani.
8. Back somersault.
9. Lazy back somersault.
10. Back Cody with full-twist.

1. Full-in back-out fliffis.
2. Barani.
3. Back somersault.
4. Rudolph.
5. Back somersault.
6. Lazy back somersault.
7. Back Cody.
8. Back with full-twist.
9. Back with full-twist.
10. Rudolph.

1. Double back somersault.
2. $2\frac{1}{4}$ forward somersault.
3. Forward cody with $\frac{1}{2}$-twist.
4. Back somersault.
5. Back with full-twist.
6. Rudolph.
7. Back somersault.
8. Back with full-twist.
9. $1\frac{3}{4}$ back somersault.
10. Back Cody.

1. $\frac{1}{2}$-in $\frac{1}{2}$-out fliffis.
2. Barani.
3. Back somersault.
4. Back with full-twist.
5. Lazy back somersault.
6. Back Cody.
7. Back somersault.
8. Back with full-twist.
9. Rudolph.
10. Rudolph.

1. Barani-out fliffis.
2. Double back somersault.
3. Back with full-twist.
4. Rudolph.
5. Back somersault.
6. Back with double-twist.
7. Back somersault.
8. Double back somersault.
9. $1\frac{1}{4}$ forward somersault.
10. Forward Cody with $\frac{1}{2}$ twist.

1. Double back somersault.
2. Back somersault.
3. Back with full-twist.
4. Back somersault.
5. Rudolph.
6. Back somersault.
7. Rudolph.
8. Back somersault.
9. Back with full-twist.
10. Back with double twist.

1. Back with full-twist.
2. Rudolph.
3. Back somersault.
4. $\frac{1}{2}$-out fliffis.
5. Rudolph.
6. Barani.
7. Back with double-twist.
8. Barani.
9. $1\frac{3}{4}$ forward somersault.
10. Barani Ball-out.

133

1. ½-out fliffis.
2. Double back somersault.
3. Rudolph.
4. Back somersault.
5. Back with full-twist.
6. Barani.
7. Back with double-twist.
8. Back somersault.
9. Back with full-twist.
10. Double back somersault.

1. Double back somersault.
2. ½-out fliffis.
3. Back with full-twist.
4. Rudolph.
5. Back somersault.
6. ¼ twisting 1¾ front somie.
7. Back Cody.
8. Back with full-twist.
9. 1¾ back somersault.
10. Back Cody with full-twist.

1. Back with double-twist.
2. 1¾ back somersault.
3. Back Cody.
4. Back with full-twist.
5. Barani.
6. Back with full-twist.
7. Back with double-twist.
8. Piked Straddle Jump.
9. Double back somersault.
10. Back with triple twist.

1. ½-out fliffis.
2. Back somersault.
3. ½-out fliffis.
4. Double back somersault.
5. Back with full-twist.
6. Barani.
7. Back somersault.
8. ½-out fliffis.
9. Double back somersault.
10. Back with double-twist.

1. ½-out fliffis.
2. Double back somersault.
3. Back with full-twist.
4. Back somersault.
5. Rudolph.
6. Back somersault.
7. Double back somersault.
8. Back with full-twist.
9. 1¾ back somersault.
10. Piked Cody.

1. 2¾ forward somersault.
2. Rudy-out ball out.
3. Back with full-twist.
4. Rudolph.
5. Back somersault.
6. Double back somersault.
7. Barani.
8. 1¾ back with ½-twist.
9. Barani Ball-out.
10. Back with double-twist.

1. Double back somersault.
2. Rudolph.
3. Back somersault.
4. Barani-out fliffis.
5. Rudolph.
6. Back with full-twist.
7. Back with double-twist.
8. Back somersault.
9. 1¾ back somersault.
10. Cody with full-twist.

1. ½-out fliffis.
2. Double back somersault.
3. Rudolph.
4. Back with full-twist.
5. Back with double-twist.
6. Barani.
7. Double back somersault.
8. Back somersault.
9. 1¾ back somersault.
10. Double Back Cody.

SWINGTIME ROUTINES

1. Triple back somersault.
2. ½-out fliffis.
3. Back somersault.
4. Back with full-twist.
5. 1¾ back somersault.
6. Double Back Cody.
7. Back somersault.
8. Back with full-twist.
9. Rudolph.
10. Double back somersault.

1. ½-out fliffis.
2. Double back somersault.
3. Rudolph.
4. Back somersault.
5. 1¾ backward somersault.
6. Back Cody with double-twist.
7. Back somersault.
8. Back with double-twist.
9. Back with full-twist.
10. Full-in, back out fliffis.

1. Full-in, ½-out fliffis.
2. Back with full-twist.
3. Double back somersault.
4. Rudolph.
5. Back somersault.
6. Back with double-twist.
7. Back somersault.
8. ½-out fliffis.
9. 1¾ backward somersault.
10. Double Back Cody.

1. ½-out fliffis.
2. Double back somersault.
3. Back with double twist.
4. Rudolph.
5. Back with full-twist.
6. ½-out fliffis.
7. Back with full-twist.
8. Back somersault.
9. 1¾ back somersault.
10. Double Back Cody.

1. Barani-out fliffis.
2. Double back somersault.
3. 2¾ forward somersault.
4. Porpus.
5. Barani Ball-out.
6. Back with full-twist.
7. 1¾ front with ½-twist.
8. Back Cody.
9. Rudolph.
10. Back with triple-twist.

1. ½-out fliffis.
2. Double back somersault.
3. Back with double-twist.
4. ½-out fliffis.
5. Double back somersault.
6. Barani.
7. Back with full-twist.
8. Back somersault.
9. 1¾ back somersault.
10. Double Back Cody.

1. ½-out fliffis.
2. ½-out fliffis.
3. Back with double-twist.
4. Double back somersault.
5. Rudolph.
6. Back with full-twist.
7. Back with double-twist.
8. Back somersault.
9. 1¾ forward somersault.
10. Rudy Ball-out.

1. Full twisting fliffis.
2. Rudolph.
3. Back with full-twist.
4. Double back somersault.
5. Double back somersault.
6. Back with double-twist.
7. Back somersault.
8. Back with full-twist.
9. 1¾ back somersault.
10. Double Back Cody.

1. Triple back somersault.
2. Barani.
3. Double back somersault.
4. Back with full-twist.
5. Double back somersault.
6. Rudolph.
7. Back with double-twist.
8. Back somersault.
9. 1¾ back somersault.
10. Double Back Cody.

1. Full-in fliffis.
2. Double back somersault.
3. ½-out fliffis.
4. Double back somersault.
5. Back with full-twist.
6. ½-out fliffis.
7. Back with double-twist.
8. Back somersault.
9. 1¾ back somersault.
10. Double Cody.

1. ½-in ½-out fliffis.
2. Double back somersault.
3. Back with double-twist.
4. Rudolph.
5. Back with full-twist.
6. Back with double-twist.
7. Back somersault.
8. ½–out fliffis.
9. 1¾ back somersault.
10. Double Back Cody.

1. Double back somersault.
2. Double back somersault.
3. Rudolph.
4. ½-out fliffis.
5. ½-in ½-out fliffis.
6. Rudolph.
7. Back with double-twist.
8. Back somersault.
9. Double back somersault.
10. Back with triple-twist.

1. Barani-in fliffis.
2. Barani-out fliffis.
3. Double back somersault.
4. 1¾ forward somersault.
5. Rudy-out ball-out.
6. Back-in, full-out fliffis.
7. Rudolph.
8. Back with full-twist.
9. 1¾ front with ½-twist.
10. Double Cody.

1. Triple back somersault.
2. ½-out fliffis.
3. Double back somersault.
4. Back with full-twist.
5. Double back somersault.
6. Rudolph.
7. Back with full-twist.
8. Back with double-twist.
9. 1¾ back somersault.
10. Double twisting cody.

1. Back with triple-twist.
2. Double back somersault.
3. Back with double-twist.
4. Back with full-twist.
5. ½-out fliffis.
6. Back with double-twist.
7. Double back somersault.
8. ½-out fliffis.
9. 1¾ back somersault.
10. Double Cody.

1. 2½ twisting fliffis.
2. Double back somersault.
3. Back-in, full-out fliffis.
4. Back with full-twist.
5. Back with double-twist.
6. ½-out fliffis.
7. Double back somersault.
8. Back with full-twist.
9. Back with double twist.
10. Double back somersault.

SWINGTIME ROUTINES

1. 2½ twisting front fliffis.
2. Double back somersault.
3. Back with double-twist.
4. Back with full-twist.
5. ½-in ½-out fliffis.
6. ½-out fliffis.
7. Rudolph.
8. Back with double-twist.
9. Back with full-twist.
10. Double twisting fliffis.

1. ½-in full-out fliffis.
2. Back-in full-out fliffis.
3. ½-out fliffis.
4. ½-in ½-out fliffis.
5. Back with double twist.
6. Double back somersault.
7. Rudolph.
8. Back with double-twist.
9. ½-out fliffis.
10. Back with triple-twist.

1. Triple back somersault.
2. Rudy-out fliffis.
3. Double back somersault.
4. ½-out fliffis.
5. Double back somersault.
6. Rudolph.
7. Back with full-twist.
8. Back with double-twist.
9. 1¾ back somersault.
10. Back Cody with triple-twist.

1. 2½ twisting fliffis.
2. Double back somersault.
3. Back with double-twist.
4. Back with full-twist.
5. ½-in ½-out fliffis.
6. ½-in ½-out fliffis.
7. Rudolph.
8. Back with double-twist.
9. ½-out fliffis.
10. Double twisting double back.

137

Trampolining and Other Activities

Because of the variety of movements and landings which are possible on the trampoline and the many ways in which the physical make-up of the body can be developed in a most enjoyable manner, this apparatus has been used by people other than trampolinists in assisting them to climb the tree to success in their own spheres.

It is not only in the field of sport that this development has taken place. Many doctors and physicians have recommended its use at rehabilitation centres across the world. Sometimes it is used as an aid to repairing and strengthening injured muscle fibres and at other times its recommendation is to give the patient an entirely new interest in life. Most recreative activities demand certain requirements which limit their adoption by the physically handicapped. At first sight I would have thought that trampolining was one of these. However, with their own specialist knowledge, the recreation officers of the physically handicapped institutes have found that the activity of trampolining is so flexible that its limitations are almost negligible.

In the pages which follow, well-known personalities in other sporting spheres tell their own stories of how the use of the trampoline has entered into their training and their lives.

*   *   *

Association Football
by DICK GRAHAM
Ex-Manager, Leyton Orient Football Club

When I was Manager of Crystal Palace Football Club, the Club Doctor, Dr. J. Reed, told me he was taking part in a trampoline course at the National Recreation Centre just a couple of miles away.

I asked him, when he had finished, to let me have his observations on this particular athletic activity because I was interested in the idea of including it in our general training routine.

Dr. Reed came to the conclusion that it would most certainly benefit a footballer, so I decided to go ahead.

The first thing I did was to ask Mr. Dennis Horne to arrange a course for our players with expert instruction. The expert instruction was imperative. Some people viewed our venture with scepticism, but I say emphatically that, having introduced trampoline work at both Crystal Palace Football Club and Charlton Athletic, I have never regretted it.

Most important, the players joined in wholeheartedly and are now quite proficient. They found it had the special advantage of being wonderful fun, quite apart from anything else.

I have found that trampoline exercises provide a challenge to the individual's determination, improves agility, timing, balance, strength and general co-ordination.

It is one of the best activities I know to rid the player of his after-match stiffness. He is able to go through a considerable limbering routine which loosens his muscles very effectively.

I am quite certain that trampoline work will eventually become a vitally important part of the modern footballer's training.

Athletics—Hitch Kick and the Trampoline
by LYNN DAVIES
Olympic, European and Commonwealth Long Jump Champion

In order to perform a good hitch kick in long jumping it is

necessary to be jumping well over 20 ft. If this distance is not achieved then the performer does not have the time in the air to move his legs.

For three years now I have been working on two and a half strides in the air or a two and a half hitch kick as it is called. As opposed to one and a half strides, it is necessary to be jumping at least 24 ft. 6 in. to perform this movement, again because of the time element.

I found that this could be performed in the following way:

(a) Bounce as high as possible on the trampoline.

(b) At the high point of the bounce begin the leg circling movements as in a hitch kick. This is a 'running in the air action'.

(c) Always rotate around the *hips* and not the knees, so producing the maximum range of movement so essential if the hitch kick is to be successful.

(d) Land in a controlled Seat Drop position.

A lot of practice at this can develop the desired movement, but it must always be practised in your long jumping as well.

The Blind

St. Vincent's School for the Blind was invited to participate in the First International Trampoline Clinic, organized in London at the National Recreation Centre, in October 1964.

Joe Senior, aged 12 years, who accompanied our P.E. mistress, Miss Stalford, showed to the admiration of all how a totally blind child can overcome his handicap on the trampoline. This was strengthened by the fact that under the tuition of a complete stranger, Joe was taught how to perform a forward somersault.

The course brought together people interested in this work to discuss and realize the problems of other instructors. In particular, it presented the problems of the physically handicapped child, and many suggestions for teaching trampoline work to such children were made.

SISTER ALOYSIUS

Rebound tumbling at our School for the Blind has proven to be a thrilling and rewarding activity. The sequence and combination of fundamental manœuvres needs little adaptation or modification for the blind. We begin by familiarizing the student with the apparatus, mounting, dismounting, walking on the bed and simple bouncing. Holding centre position, maintaining body alignment and developing a reliable direction sense are the chief obstacles for the blind beginner. However, skill quickly develops with verbal correction and suggestion. Special markings or sound signals to indicate right and left or centre, as yet have not been necessary or desirable. Class members are spotted around the frame as a safeguard for the performer. There is a natural reluctance of the blind child to ignore the wisdom of maintaining the security of contact with Mother Earth and this sometimes reflects itself in a tenseness and rigidity of movement. Often we find that the young totally blind child will require persistent encouragement to progress beyond the normal walking stage to running, skipping and jumping. When the student masters the basic skill of rebound tumbling, he enjoys the thrill of aerial manœuvre without undue apprehension to limit his full and free performance. The action of the bouncing bed demands muscle co-ordination and rhythm, thus encouraging the development of agility and ease of motor function. In its unique manner the apparatus stimulates action and provides vigorous exercise and body conditioning within a specific area which is known to the blind child. There have been noticeable improvements in the ability of our youngsters to maintain centre and control balance. We have a few children who have severe problems of co-ordination and balance and for some of these students the improvement in control has been quite remarkable.

ROBERT MEALEY, *P.E.I. Washington State School for the Blind in Vancouver, Washington.*

Trampolining for the Competitive Cyclist

by BILL DODDS

Senior South East London British Cycling Federation Coach,
G.L.C. Senior Cycling Coach and England Team Manager

Some four years ago I had a problem on my hands. The racing cyclists I was training and coaching were in the gymnasium one evening a week to maintain some of the fitness they had worked for so hard during the winter months. Having competed in races sometimes over 100 miles the previous day, I had to make sure that the workout would not be too hard or in any way uninteresting, and yet at the same time be of benefit to their racing. There were many games which I used to give the programme a good variety; basketball, volleyball, badminton, handball and gymnastics, both formal and informal. Most of my riders tried most of the activities but there were always a few who found gymnastics too hard for them, or playing ball games not to their liking. So, I always tried anything new I thought would help my riders. Then I attended an I.L.E.A. teachers' course on Trampoline-Tumbling run by Ted Blake and Pat Winkle. This was what I had been looking for. I soon realized the many advantages this type of work could have for the racing cyclists. I wanted to know if it had any adverse effect on the riders. The only way to find out was to learn to perform for myself, which I did. I also became a qualified trampoline coach so that I could train the riders myself. Both track and road riders are now using the trampoline during the summer months and some use it all the year round as part of their training programme. Riders such as Keith Butler, the ex-British Professional Champion, Empire Medallist John Clarey of the Cambrian Wheelers Woolwich Cycling Club and Mick Ballard of the West Kent Road Club, a rider who has ridden over 110 time-trial cycle races of 25 miles total distance inside one hour. They all find the trampoline a great way to spend their gymnasium training time. We have quite a job to get them off! Many of the up and coming riders are also taking to the trampoline. Riders such as Reg Smith of the London Coureurs, and John Savage of the Woolwich Cycling Club both show great promise as riders and trampoline performers. The great thing about the trampoline is not the advantages you can get from it but the fun of performing on it even after a 100-miles-plus race the day before. A final summary of the benefits of trampolining for the competitive cyclist is the development of neuromuscular co-ordination, circulo-respiratory efficiency, courage, confidence, the awareness of where one is when performing some very demanding exercise or combination of exercises and the development of the power to overcome the next challenge to oneself.

Trampolining Cosmonauts

Right from the very early days when the trampoline was first used commercially, the flyers in America used this apparatus in their training programme. With the advancements made in flying and the present space flight programme, many techniques have changed since those early days but the trampoline still remains as an important piece of flight training equipment. Cosmonauts are able to obtain simple delayed flights where certain aerial manœuvres are made possible. In this way space orientation can be practised quite easily at any time.

Two pictures in this book show trampolines installed at the space training centres of the world's two most advanced countries in space flight—Russia and America.

Trampolining for the Diver
by WALLY ORNER
Coach to Brian Phelps

There is no doubt in my mind that the trampoline is the greatest aid to divers since the development of the springboard, but unfortunately it is sadly neglected by most British divers—and coaches! There are some very obvious benefits.

On the trampoline, the diver can learn new dives as it allows landing in several controllable attitudes around the body in addition to the feet, whereas only straight body-vertical entries are comfortable into water.

143

In conjunction with bathside 'work-ups' the constituents of the dive can be broken into sections to an extent where no problems need bar progress.

As trampolines are normally used in gymnasia or halls, the use of aids to learning such as somersaulting and twisting belts is a far more practical proposition than use of such apparatus over a diving board in most pools.

'Work-ups' from the bathside have certain limitations which can be largely eliminated on the trampoline in that it can add several fractions of somersault to a series of landings which would be most uncomfortable or discouraging on water, e.g. prone or supine. Dives can be built up in fractions by successive use of 'work-ups' from the bathside and on the trampoline, greatly speeding the learning process as confidence is maintained by painless sequence of simple parts of the whole movement.

Among other obvious benefits are the ability to train for longer periods in the greater comfort of a hall in a 'dressed' condition or 'working up heat', not normally possible in cold and draughty pools. Repetition of movements in more rapid succession than is normally possible from a diving board can lead to faster learning, and several successive attempts at any movement on a trampoline before a diver dismounts avoid many distractions which affect divers in the usual queue for a diving board.

All this, in relation to trampoline work specifically for divers, gets divers disciplined to the special needs and limitations of trampolining, and can add a further sport by learning a series of eight to ten simple and more advanced stunts and engaging in 'rebound tumbling' competition. This can offer greater scope for aerial acrobatics, add a new dimension to their skills in providing them with improved fitness and, less obviously, the enhanced self-correction capacity which is acquired in rebound tumbling will help to minimize the effects of poor take-off in diving to an extent that simply diving can never do.

Films and Stunt Men

The trampoline and the Mini-Tramp have been used quite extensively by the film industry. The trampolines are not always seen by the audience but they are there behind the scenery or dug into the ground. Stunt men land on them, jump from them and are propelled at various angles by them. When you see a person fall from a height having been shot, invariably below him is a trampoline or a pile of mattresses to ensure a safe landing. Soldiers blown into the air during battle scenes have most probably bounced from Mini-Tramps at the same time as the explosions. This is precisely what happened in the film *Shenandoah*. Ronnie Rondell, the stunt man, blew up whilst carrying a supply of ammunition and the resultant somersault through the air was from a Mini-Tramp. You may remember the scene.

Lorne Janes somersaulted over Doris Day's head into a pool during the film *Move Over, Darling*. He also landed in the arms of a statue from one of his leaps in *It's a Mad, Mad, Mad, Mad World*. If you saw the film *What a Way to Go*, you may recall Bob Mitchum's tussle with a bull resulting with Bob flying through the barn wall. This again was Lorne being propelled from a trampoline.

Another unusual effect which was obtained through the use of a trampoline was in the 'Flubber' series. A basketball team wearing boots with the special 'Flubber' soles were able to jump around at such a height that their opponents could not reach the ball. This was possible not because of the composition of the boots but because a long trampoline was incorporated as part of the flooring.

Other films which come to mind where a trampoline or Mini-Tramps were used are *From Russia With Love*, *Follow that Fire*, *Trapeze*, *The Greatest Show on Earth*, *How the West was Won* and *Sargent's 3*.

The Physically Handicapped
by RALPH DIAPHER
P.E. Organizer, Newport, Mon.

The ways in which the trampoline is used in conjunction with the physically handicapped are many and varied. In making a

K   145

choice as to which way to show the work achieved in this field, I decided to give an example of one person from South Wales.

A young man I have been coaching was born without hands, with only one leg and very poor eyesight, but, fortunately with tremendous spirit and well-above-average intelligence. His attitude to physical challenges is that he can do almost anything a normal young man can do. I would go further in saying that his physical achievements are very much above average.

He joined the Newport Trampoline Club as one of its first members and soon mastered all the basic jumps and drops, progressing within four sessions to perform a reasonable front somersault. His total trampolining time to reach this stage could not have exceeded 80 minutes. My main concern was trying to curb his enthusiasm to attempt more difficult movements. When not on the trampoline at the gym he used to enjoy himself on other items of equipment including the trampette and vaulting over the box.

Swimming
by BILL LUDGROVE
Father and coach to Linda Ludgrove, International Back-stroke Star and World Record Breaker

I started trampolining with Linda about four years ago. We made tremendous use of this activity particularly since we were able to get on the trampolines at Crystal Palace. Attending a C.C.P.R. Course for trampolining was a tremendous boost to Linda and her general physical fitness improved. We could get fit in the water but we now needed a sort of land conditioner to supplement this. I found that the trampoline programme Linda was put through was a tremendous help.

We continued on our own after this and made great strides, mostly in what we call the loosening-up exercises for stretching the ankles. We found the Knee Drop most useful for this. I found that by getting Linda to do somersaults on the trampoline she could tuck up more in her somersault turn. Another activity we did was to put the trampoline about 6 ft. away from

146

the wall bars so that Linda practised her back stroke starts on to the trampoline. This was quite an achievement because after a week we could move the trampoline out to about 10 ft. and Linda could still land in the middle of it, so there must have been some improvement in her take-off.

We started trampolining because one gets a bit stale out of the water. Running gets monotonous and swimmers do not like running anyway. Once they get adapted to the water, swimmers do not like land training; they want to stay in the water. When we tried trampolining, it was new and a bit different. I found I could get my swimmers' pulse rates up while they were enjoying the work. I believe that if they enjoy what they are doing then we are getting somewhere.

In swimming, we measure the amount of work being done by feeling the pulse rate. I was very much surprised that after about five minutes on the trampoline, even just bouncing up and down and doing the occasional Knee Drop and somersault, the pulse rates of my swimmers went up to 180°–190°, which is equivalent to a good 440 yd. swim. To achieve this without getting wet, I would normally have to send the swimmers on a run. I am not so keen on swimmers running because they lose quite a lot of flexibility of the ankles, particularly as they bang down on a hard road. This does not happen on the trampoline since the bed gives and the bouncer goes down with it. Also, there are many basic movements which can be performed to take the weight off their feet for a while.

I think it is a necessary job that we have got to keep the kids happy while they are training and if trampolining makes their pulse rate rise and, at the same time, they enjoy themselves, then we are doing something good.

11

History

In Britain, a physical education specialist by the name of Ted Blake was rather interested in watching films of the new American sport of trampolining. Information and literature about the sport were non-existent in this country and so Ted set himself the task of obtaining all the information he could. His interest rapidly increased as more details became available. With Ted's background of physical education and his fertile brain it did not take him long to realize the wonderful effect this activity had on the human body. It was just what he wanted for his boys at Loxford School, Ilford, Essex; a new activity with an unlimited range of muscular co-ordination, rapid success and built-in safety precautions. No longer did age, sex, physical make-up, determine whether or not participation was possible. Here was a sport for everyone.

After many failures at trying to get his local education authority to import a trampoline for school use, Ted finally saw an advertisement in a magazine stating that there was a second-hand trampoline for sale. He immediately contacted his Physical Education Organizer and again put forward his request. This time there was a better response. Since so much money was involved, the only possibility would be if the Youth Organizer was willing to share in the use and expense of such an undertaking. Trampolining and diving, it was thought, were very much akin and so the Ilford Diving Club was approached to see if they were interested in using the apparatus for part of their training. The invitation was eagerly accepted and so a visit to the vendors was arranged. On the appointed day in 1949, four men travelled together full of hope and expectations. They were Harry Crabtree, County Physical Education Organizer; Ken Stagg, Youth Officer; Cyril Laxton, Olympic Diving Coach, and Ted Blake, the brains and force behind the whole venture. After a great deal of haggling about the price (one would have thought they were all in a Persian market), an agreement was reached and there was at least one very happy man.

Months of enjoyable, but at the same time strenuous, physical and mental activity followed. The favourite piece of gymnastic apparatus at Loxford School was undoubtedly the trampoline. Since very little literature was available at the time, many movements had to be learned through a great deal of forethought and trial and error. Even so, because of the careful supervision and intelligent procedures insisted upon, the learning stages were accident-free. Requests to give demonstrations at various functions, including the 1951 Festival of Britain, rolled in steadily and the Ilford Boys and their trampoline became well-known all over the country. Even the Ilford Diving Club's performance in competitions improved. No longer was just a place in the finals of the National Championships a great achievement; they began to fill the first three places! Although this did not happen all in one year or in the same type of competition, their numbers in the finals increased.

In 1956 Ted Blake became a managing director of a branch of the Nissen Trampoline Co. Ltd. which was set up in England to cope with the British and European markets. The original English headquarters had to be within easy reach of its components and since the early trampoline beds were only made from solid sheets of canvas or a combination of canvas and nylon, what could be better than moving in and taking over part of a canvas manufacturer's buildings in Romford. The county of Essex being virtually responsible for starting trampolining in this country, and having experienced its benefits, began to purchase this apparatus for its other schools. London University and Rochdale Education Committee soon followed suit. Courses were organized for teachers all over the country and certificates were awarded to those passing certain tests. The very first Open Trampoline Competition to be held in this country was at a water carnival organized by the Ilford Diving Club in 1957. The winner on this occasion was an Ilford diver by the name of Mick Forge. Since this was an open competition it could be said that Mick was the first ever British trampoline champion.

The first man to form a trampoline association in Great Britain was David Webster, a senior technical representative of the Scottish Council of Physical Recreation. This was the Scottish Trampoline Association which eventually merged with the Scottish Amateur Gymnastic Association. However, on the 18th November 1959, five physical education specialists with a particular interest in trampolining met together informally at a private house in Gidea Park, Essex, for the purpose of setting up a committee to arrange competitions at national level. These five founder members of the Amateur Gymnastic Association Trampolining Committee were Ted Blake, managing director of the Nissen Company; Jack Garstang, assistant director of physical education at Regent St. Polytechnical College; Geoff Elliott, the international pole vaulter and one-time Amateur Athletic Association team captain; Syd Aaron, senior P.E. lecturer at Cardiff Training College, and myself. Sitting around the fire until the early hours of the morning, we constructed the original constitution for the association, rules and regulations for competitions and the very first set routine for a National Championship—in fact the first official National Championship in Europe. Everyone contributed something towards the compulsory routine and it looked rather weird to see grown men jumping up and down on the floor throwing their bodies around trying to imagine they were bouncing on a trampoline. This was the only way in which we could feel whether all the suggested movements would flow smoothly together since a practice trampoline was not at hand. The ultimate concoction finished up as the following nine-bounce routine (this should have been an eight-bounce routine but we did not count correctly):

1. Tuck Jump.
2. Pike Jump.
3. Back somersault tucked.
4. Knee Drop.
5. Front somersault tucked.

6. Seat Drop.
7. Swivel Hips.
8. Roller.
9. To feet.

In the early days we used to find that more divers took an interest in trampolining since the individual movements performed in the two sports were very similar. Multiple somersaults and twisting somersaults were the basic movements of the divers and it was easy for them to transfer, whereas the gymnast, in the main, was still playing with these movements on the floor. This was borne out when the entries came in for our first National Championships which were held at the R.A.F. Sports Arena, Stanmore Park, Middlesex, in conjunction with the British Amateur Gymnastic Association's Vaulting and Agility Championships. The championships were divided into four competitions: Men, Women, Boys under 16 and Girls under 16. Just over sixty entries were received of which the majority were from divers. On the official side, we decided to interest as many people as possible and, therefore, we asked P.E. lecturers, diving judges and coaches to perform these services.

I am setting out below the results of these championships because they are historic—and also there are some well-known names amongst the competitors which you may recognize.

First National Trampoline Championships, 1959

Men

Name	Set	Vol.	Total	Position
Brian Phelps	8·55	8·45	17·00	1st
John Ley	8·20	7·80	16·00	2nd
Peter Quinney	7·65	7·70	15·35	3rd
Randall Bevan	6·90	8·40	15·30	4th
Alan Faires	8·40	6·00	14·40	5th
John Candler	5·70	7·05	12·75	6th
Nicky Ruoss	6·50	6·00	12·50	7th

Of these competitors, Peter Quinney and Randall Bevan were the only two who were not divers. However, both of them became British Champions in later years; Peter in 1960 and Randall in 1961 and 1962. As everyone knows, Brian Phelps became Britain's greatest diver when he won the European Highboard Championships in 1958 and 1962 and also took the bronze medal at the 1960 Olympic Games in Rome. With his background knowledge and experience gained through diving and trampolining, John Ley has become one of our most successful coaches. His team of girls has always put up a good show at the championships and Lynda Ball was the British Junior Champion in 1962, second in the First World Championships in 1964, British Ladies Champion in 1965, fourth in the 1965 and 1966 World Championships and British Champion again in 1966. John Candler became an international diver representing Great Britain at the 1960 and 1964 Olympic Games and World Professional Champion in 1966. Nicky Ruoss also became one of the country's leading divers.

WOMEN

Name	Set	Vol.	Total	Position
Marion Watson	7·70	6·55	14·25	1st
Linda Hutton	4·35	4·50	8·85	2nd
Jean Gill	3·15	5·60	8·75	3rd
Ann Dearlove	2·75	3·10	5·75	4th
Jean Garstang	3·15	2·00	5·15	5th
Ann Taber	1·40	3·70	5·10	6th
Valerie Steer	2·75	1·50	4·25	7th

As can be seen from the marks, with the exception of Marion Watson, the ladies had a great deal of difficulty with the swing-time routines. Here again we had a whole string of divers but the performing of one movement immediately after another was different from diving and this called for extra skill. Only Marion had this extra skill and control which again came to the fore when she won the British Diving Championships in 1958.

Phelps again won the Boys' Championship. By comparing his marks in the two competitions, it can be seen that he was a safe and consistent performer. One of the main reasons why the divers always showed so well was because of their impeccable style. Naturally divers are style-conscious and this certainly stood them in good stead for this type of competition.

BOYS UNDER 16

Name	Set	Vol.	Total	Position
Brian Phelps	8·35	8·50	16·85	1st
	6·15	5·80	11·95	2nd
	5·60	5·10	10·70	3rd
	5·50	5·05	10·55	4th
	4·50	4·25	8·75	5th
	4·60	3·65	8·25	6th
	4·65	3·50	8·15	7th

Margaret Austen, one of Britain's top divers at the time, proved once again that the training and experience of the divers were extremely good grounding for trampolining.

GIRLS UNDER 16

Name	Set	Vol.	Total	Position
Margaret Austen	3·00	4·15	7·15	1st
Marion Austen	2·75	4·10	6·85	2nd
	2·85	2·20	5·05	3rd
	2·20	2·50	4·70	4th

Since trampolining outside the United States of America was in its infancy there were no international meetings of any kind. Therefore, the main tasks of the committee at this stage were levelled at organizing National Championships, setting up judging, coaching and proficiency awards and importing as much information as possible on trampolining from the United States. On Saturday, 23rd January 1960, we organized the very first International Trampoline Competition in conjunction with an Olympic gymnastic match between England and Wales, at the Wembley Town Hall. Since this was our very first try-out at staging this type of competition, we allowed only one competitor from each country. Peter Quinney represented England while Randall Bevan, the winner of the competition, bounced for Wales.

Our second National Championships were also held at the R.A.F. Sports Arena, Stanmore, and included an additional competition for Veterans; this was open to anyone over 35 years of age. But even with this addition we did not have as many competitors as for the first championships. Each section had its very own compulsory routine instead of the same routine performed by all as was the case the year before. The only exception to this was for the Veterans where the competitors could perform two voluntary routines. The Boys' event accumulated the greatest number of competitors with eighteen. The Men's competition totalled twelve entries, the Girls' eleven, the Women's six and the Veterans two. This fall in competition numbers was put down to two factors. One was because of the individual compulsory routines which, naturally, were far more difficult than before, and secondly, that at the time of the championships the diving fraternity had a previous engagement which meant that there were practically no entries from the divers, especially not the best of them. Because of the rapid interest in this new sport, other companies began to manufacture the apparatus and cash-in on its popularity. This caused rather a disturbance because the word 'Trampoline' was a registered trade name used by the inventors, Nissen Trampoline Co., Ltd. and, therefore, could not be used as a general term for all companies or as the name for a sport. It was noticeable that the movements performed on the trampoline were very similar to those performed on the ground for the American sport of tumbling. Since on the trampoline the performer obtained a rebound from the apparatus between each stunt there could be no better name for the sport than Rebound Tumbling. So towards the end of 1959 the word 'Trampoline' was dropped and the new term 'Rebound Tumbling' took its place.

The full results of the Second National Rebound Tumbling Championships, as they were called, seem to have been lost for ever in the changes of time; new official offices taken over, prominent people moving and destroying accumulated papers. However the winners' names have been recorded and are as follows:

SECOND NATIONAL REBOUND TUMBLING CHAMPIONSHIPS,
1960

1st   Peter Quinney
2nd   Randall Bevan

Most people were pleased to see Peter win because of the

greater degree of difficulty he showed in the content of his voluntary routine. The one thing that could have let him down was his style. Randall gave Peter a good run for his title and they were to do battle many times later in various contests.

WOMEN	1st	Jackie Allen
BOYS	1st	H. Perry
GIRLS	1st	S. Hawtin
VETERANS	1st	Syd Aaron
	2nd	Nick Carter

The innovation of the Veterans' event only attracted two entries but a very interesting contest took place. The first performer failed to complete his routine, which according to the rules and regulations in operation at that time meant that only a zero score could be awarded. The title was now left wide open for the only other performer to accept. Over-confidence prevailed and he too failed to complete his routine. The second bounce-off between these two performers resulted in a win for Syd Aaron.

At a committee meeting to discuss the arrangements for these second National Championships a great deal of time was spent considering voluntary routines. Even at this early stage of top competition work in Britain, the matter of competitors submitting a written routine was debated. Five years later the leading representatives from all over the world met to decide the same topic when compiling universal rules for all international matches. The decision was made that no voluntary routine needed to be handed to the referee before the competition. However, to make certain that a presentable standard of performance was shown at the championships, it was announced that two full marks would be deducted for each free bounce appearing in a routine!

Because of such a poor entry for the 1960 Nationals, we felt that perhaps we were trying to push the sport and competitors too hard by making them all perform eight-bounce routines irrespective of the section they had entered. We were trying to catch up with the Americans and get our competitors on a parallel with their methods. Well, we learnt our lesson and we paid the price.

On 18th March 1961, the Kent County Schools' Rebound Tumbling Association held their first ever county championships at the Cray Valley Technical High School for Boys. This is thought to be the first county championships for schools to be held in the whole of Great Britain and the force behind this venture came from the assistant P.E. adviser for that county, Mr. A. J. G. Hopkins. It was some years later in 1964 that other school associations were set up and championships held.

The introductory phase of the trampoline into the world of gymnastics was no smooth journey. It was looked upon by some with the suspicion of the unknown. Others scorned the arrival of a new piece of apparatus into the serenity of an ancient society. At first, spurious excuses were found to exile this intruder. The most common of these was that the suspension system used for the trampoline would help to kill natural spring and, this being the case, the whole of vaulting and agility exercises would suffer. As it happened, quite the reverse was to occur. It was noticeable that the leg muslces of the bouncers became more and more powerful. As the sport progressed, trampolinists took their movements to the floor and included them into tumbling sequences. Even young boys and girls now perform such movements as consecutive hollow-back somersaults; full-twisting and double-twisting somersaults. The men have taken this a stage further and included double somersaults in their routines! The old saying that trampoline work kills natural spring has certainly been disproved. The fact is that trampolining goes a long way towards the acquisition of a much stronger, more powerful take-off. Stunt-wise the trampolinists, although very much the babies of the sport, have already progressed beyond the performances of the pure gymnasts. However, let us return to the early history once more before we deviate too far from the original chronological order of events.

For the 1961 National Championships, we left the number of bounces for the Men competitors at eight but reduced this to six bounces for the Women's, Boys' and Girls' events. The response was the best so far: 16 entries from the Girls; 24 from the Women; 39 from the Boys and 24 from the Men.

THIRD NATIONAL REBOUND TUMBLING CHAMPIONSHIPS, 1961

BOYS UNDER 16

Name	Total	Position
T. Evans	17·25	1
M. Williams	17·25	2
A. Daly	17·00	3
J. Steadman	16·50	4
R. Boxer	15·50	5
M. Humphrey	15·25	6

GIRLS UNDER 16

Name	Total	Position
M. Clee	17·25	1
A. Miller	15·50	2
J. Pigrome	14·50	3
L. Ball	14·25	4
P. Collier	14·25	5
S. Hawtin	14·25	6

WOMEN

Name	Set	Vol.	Total	Position
Jackie Allen	8·75	7·50	16·25	1
Mary Chamberlaine	7·50	7·75	15·25	2
Marilyn Clee	7·50	7·00	14·50	3
Linda Hutton	6·75	7·50	14·25	4
Anne Miller	7·50	6·25	13·75	5
Elizabeth Hunter	7·00	6·00	13·00	6

MEN (Qualifying Round)

Name	Set	Vol.	Total	Position
Len Rapkins	8·25	7·25	15·50	1
David Smith	7·75	7·50	15·25	2
Peter Bartlett	7·50	7·50	15·00	3
Randall Bevan	8·25	5·50	13·75	4
Malcolm Clarke	7·00	6·00	13·00	5
Kevin Clarke	6·75	5·75	12·50	6

This was the order of the Men's competition after the qualifying rounds. When the competitors met again they would all begin from scratch, the points scored in the preliminary rounds not being carried forward to the finals.

There was something special about that year's competitions. Firstly, the venue was at the Wembley Town Hall; and then the six finalists in the Men's section were to compete amid the grandeur of the Royal Albert Hall together with the finalists of the Men's and Women's Olympic Gymnastics Championships. Never before in the whole history of modern gymnastics in Britain had a championship taken place under the roof of such an amphitheatre. Here was the beginning of the revival of Olympic gymnastics in this country and the forerunner of many great trampoline matches. To conclude the championships in a befitting manner there was a fanfare of trumpets by the Household Cavalry prior to the awarding of the trophies by the Earl of Gainsborough. Indeed a most memorable occasion. All this would not have been possible if it had not been for the sport of gymnastics having its very first sponsor in Odhams Press.

The date chosen for these finals was Saturday, 25th March! Our first really big chance to show a vast audience our sport, since it was also being televised, and it had to clash with that mecca of steeplechasing, the 'Grand National', also being televised! How on earth could we hope to entice new spectators with such a counter attraction? Somehow the miracle happened —6,000 spectators attended the Royal Albert Hall that day.

MEN (Final Round)

Name	Set	Vol.	Total	Position
Randall Bevan	8·0	9·10	17·10	1
Len Rapkins	8·0	7·50	15·50	2
Peter Bartlett	7·0	8·25	15·25	3
David Smith	6·0	8·75	14·75	4
Malcolm Clarke	6·0	6·00	12·00	5
Kevin Clarke	7·0	2·00	9·00	6

Besides being a most historic championship because of the change of venues, the Men finalists competing at the Royal Albert Hall and all the pomp and circumstance, there was one other feature. It became noticeable that rebound tumbling was developing its own type of sportsmen. Where divers used to play a great part in dominating all trampoline competitions, they now began to drop by the wayside. Even with the greatest number of competitors so far recorded only four were divers—Len Rapkins who took second place in the Men's competition and three Ilford Diving Club members in the Boys' contest. As the following years will show, the number of divers competing at national level can be counted on one hand. Those who persisted with trampolining were really in the process of changing sports and becoming converts.

The year of 1961 really was a most historic one for rebound tumbling. It was on 11th November of that year that the first ever international competition took place between two foreign countries. A British team was invited to compete against a West German team as part of the programme for the German Polizei Sportschau held at the Ostseehallein, Kiel. This really was a grand occasion with international contests of indoor athletics, ballroom dancing and rebound tumbling, combined with gymnastics, roller skating, tug-of-war and dogs playing football. Our expenses were paid by the Kiel Police Sports Association who also made all the arrangements. It was quite an experience being driven around in a police van amid stares of suspicion from the onlookers; I only hope we did not leave them with the wrong impression. However, we really are indebted to the West German police for honouring us with this memorable occasion.

The team chosen to represent Great Britain consisted of Randall Bevan, Len Rapkins, Brian Phelps, Pat Winkle and Peter Quinney with Rob Walker as team manager and myself as coach-cum-judge. Our opposition was completely unknown to us, as we were to them. Everyone awaited the day of the competition eagerly in order to see just how far another country had progressed. We felt a certain pride in our hearts because we had been bouncing longer than any other European country and so we thought that we should have the edge over our opposition. The day finally arrived with both teams looking immaculately dressed, a credit to each country. 9,000 spectators packed the sports hall on the Saturday afternoon in order to watch the compulsory routines. The teams bounced alternately, beginning with the Germans. Although five men competed for each team it was agreed that only the best four in each case counted in the final reckoning. It was quite a coincidence that each team included two international divers in their ranks. The Germans were, without doubt, far superior so far as style was concerned and we could see that our only chance would be to make up any deficit by using difficulty in the two voluntary routines to be performed in the evening.

Again 9,000 spectators attended for the evening's competitions. Both German and British television organizations were there to give the rebound tumbling match adequate coverage for both countries. As the competition progressed it became apparent that the Germans' theme tune was, 'Anything you can do I can do better.' It seemed that each competitor who stepped forward tried to better the performance of the last bouncer, the Germans topping our boys each time. The style of the German boys was a treat to watch and it taught us the lesson that one has not just to do the difficult work but perform neatly at the same time.

Roland Schillinger, the West German champion at the time, was most consistent. The marks for his three routines were 9·80, 9·90 and 9·90, the nearest thing to maximum points. In fact I did award a mark of 10 for his final routine but this was eliminated together with a mark of 9·90 in order to find the average. The individual scores for this competition were as follows:

West Germany	*Compulsory*	*1st Vol.*	*2nd Vol.*	*Total*
1. Roland Schillinger	9·80	9·90	9·90	29·60
2. Joachim Scherf	9·75	9·75	9·80	29·30
3. Horst Schlindwein	9·20	9·60	9·50	28·30
4. Gunter Hoog	9·25	9·35	9·55	28·15
5. W. Luft	9·55	8·20	9·60	27·35

	142·70
W. Luft's score was not included since only the best four were to count	27·35
	Final score 115·35

	Great Britain	Compulsory	1st Vol.	2nd Vol.	Total
1.	Brian Phelps	9·30	9·35	9·45	28·10
2.	Peter Quinney	9·15	9·30	9·25	27·70
3.	Leonard Rapkins	8·90	9·40	9·40	27·70
4.	Patrick Winkle	9·05	9·20	9·30	27·55
5.	Randall Bevan	9·10	9·05	9·05	27·20

	138·25
Randall Bevan's score was not included since only the best four were to count	27·20
Final score	111·05

The competitors who were also divers came first and second in the West German team and first in the British team, showing once again that their grounding for diving was ideal for rebound tumbling. One further interesting point which was borne out at this competition was the fact that the top four German performers were all coached by the same man, Dr. Heinz Braecklein of Freiburg University, the bouncers themselves all being students at the same university. Because of this arrangement it was possible for their national team to train together regularly under Germany's top coach, a necessity which we could not afford. Our team came from as far apart as Aldershot to Loughborough and London to Cardiff. This was not an excuse for our team losing because we came away feeling that with more style our boys could hold their own against anyone in Europe, but it does show that training together is a great asset for motivating competitors.

1962 was like a shot in the arm for trampolining. More and more people were clamouring to learn about this sport and competitions were being held all over the country. Clubs and areas held their own championships; there were inter-club competitions, inter-collegiate matches and invitation meetings open to the top bouncers in the country. In Europe it was the same story. The beginnings of European Championships sprang up, the first being held on 19th May in Ludwigshaven, Germany. Representing Great Britain was Pat Winkle, a sergeant instructor of the Army Physical Training Corps, and already one of our international team which competed against West Germany in Kiel the previous year.

Trampolining was at last beginning to receive international status since this year also saw the inauguration of a new competition for which a trophy known as the 'Grand European Cup' was presented to the champion man trampolinist of Europe. The date of this unofficial European Championship was on 10th November 1962. Two competitors were invited from each of the European countries and Pat Winkle and Chris Netherton, at this time a new boy, represented England. The result published was:

1st	Hoog	Germany (Champion of Europe)	29·1
2nd {	Winkle	Great Britain	28·5
	Schere	Germany	28·5
4th	Bachler	Switzerland	28·2
5th	Netherton	Great Britain	28·0

Other countries competing were Austria, Denmark, Holland, Italy and Sweden.

Because of the growing interest in the sport and because the term 'trampolining' was being used more than 'rebound tumbling', the name for the sport reverted to its original title of 'trampolining'.

NATIONAL TRAMPOLINE CHAMPIONSHIPS, 1962
PRELIMINARIES

MEN

Name	Set	Vol.	Total	Position
Pat Winkle	9·25	8·75	18·00	1
David Smith	8·00	7·50	15·50	2
Brian Phelps	7·50	7·50	15·00	} 3
Randall Bevan	8·00	7·00	15·00	
Len Rapkins	7·50	7·25	14·75	5

LADIES

Name	Set	Vol.	Total	Position
Mary Chamberlaine	7·50	7·50	15·00	1
Francis McLeod	7·50	6·00	13·50	} 2
Cpl. Joyce Thomas	6·50	7·00	13·50	
Elizabeth Hunter	7·00	6·25	13·25	4
Yvonne Horne	7·50	5·50	13·00	5

MEN'S FINAL

Name	Set	Vol.	Total	Position
Randall Bevan	9·00	8·50	17·50	1
David Smith	8·75	8·50	17·25	2
Len Rapkins	8·25	7·65	15·90	3
Chris Netherton	7·50	7·00	14·50	4
Pat Winkle	9·50	3·00	12·50	5

LADIES' FINAL

Name	Set	Vol.	Total	Position
Yvonne Horne	8·50	7·75	16·25	1
Francis McLeod	8·00	8·00	16·00	2
Joyce Thomas	7·50	8·25	15·75	} 3
Elizabeth Hunter	7·50	8·25	15·75	
Mary Chamberlaine	7·00	8·00	15·00	5

Because the sport set up its own governing body in 1965, the B.A.G.A. discarded all the papers and results of the trampoline competitions and so only the names of the winners in the Junior sections are recorded.

Boys' Final	1st	J. Steadman
Girls' Final	1st	Lynda Ball

In the Men's Final, Brian Phelps withdrew from the competition allowing Chris Netherton, who was in sixth position, to compete. Because the Men and Women had to take part in two contests before deciding who was the champion of Great Britain, the trampoline committee agreed in future to carry over to the finals the marks awarded in the preliminary rounds. This would produce the best all-round and consistent performer.

Each year the European countries were striving for more and more international competitions. The largest meeting to date came in May of 1963 but, before this, England began the year with the finals of the National Championships. The preliminary competitions for 1963 were held at the Spence Street Baths, Leicester, on 15th December 1962.

NATIONAL TRAMPOLINE CHAMPIONSHIPS, 1963
BOYS

Name	Preliminary	Final	Position
David Curtis	19·05	38·05	1
S. Wood	18·80	37·65	2
M. McCarthy	18·85	37·55	3
Roland Farlie	18·40	36·30	4
L. Jones	18·15	36·25	5

GIRLS

Name	Preliminary	Final	Position
S. Wills	18·90	37·10	1
P. Collier	18·35	36·00	2
Sheila Hawtin	18·00	35·30	3
Yvonne Ireland	17·85	35·20	4
Jill Taylor	17·45	34·30	5

At this time there was a great undercurrent of dissatisfaction raging in the world of British trampolining. After the preliminary contests in Leicester, the majority of the trampoline committee members handed their resignations in to the secretary of the B.A.G.A., to take effect after the finals at the Albert Hall. At the same time it was announced that the British Trampoline Association had already been formed to take control of the sport. The timing was most unfortunate because of the pending international matches.

The finals of the Men's and Women's competitions were held on 16th February 1963 at the Royal Albert Hall:

LADIES

Name	Preliminary	Set	Vol.	Total	Position
Mary Chamberlaine	19·25	9·05	9·35	37·65	1
Lynda Ball	18·55	8·55	8·90	36·55	2
Margaret Mills	18·75	8·45	8·90	36·10	3
Joyce Thomas	18·35	8·75	9·00	36·10	3
Jacquie Allan	18·35	8·40	8·95	35·70	5

MEN

Name	Preliminary	Set	Vol.	Total	Position
Pat Winkle	19·20	9·20	9·45	37·85	1
David Smith	19·05	9·30	9·35	37·70	2
Randall Bevan	19·20	9·15	9·30	37·65	3
Alex Howden	18·70	9·00	9·25	36·95	4
Mike Williams	18·40	9·00	—	27·40	5

On March 15th and 16th we were allowed to put on an international match between England and Wales at the A.A.A. Indoor Championships at the Empire Pool, Wembley. This was an experiment to get trampolining before the eyes of the public and also a good excuse to organize an international competition. One man and one woman represented each country and their combined scores produced the result. For England, Pat Winkle and Mary Chamberlaine were chosen and, for Wales, Randall Bevan and Jacquie Allan.

On the Friday night each competitor executed two different voluntary routines with the following result:

Name	Country	First Voluntary Points				Total
1. Jacquie Allen	Wales	8·7	8·6	8·7	7·9	8·70
2. Mary Chamberlaine	England	9·2	9·2	8·9	9·2	9·20
3. Randall Bevan	Wales	9·2	9·2	9·4	9·6	9·30
4. Pat Winkle	England	9·6	9·4	9·4	9·6	9·50

Name	Country	Second Voluntary Points				Total
1. Jacquie Allen	Wales	9·3	9·1	9·1	8·9	9·10
2. Mary Chamberlaine	England	9·1	9·0	9·0	8·9	9·00
3. Randall Bevan	Wales	9·4	9·1	9·2	9·3	9·25
4. Pat Winkle	England	9·1	9·0	9·5	9·5	9·30

Result: ENGLAND 37·00   WALES 36·35

This seemed to meet with some measure of success both from the audience and the organizers since we were asked to appear on the Saturday afternoon. Because of the amount of time allocated only one voluntary routine was performed.

165

Name	Country	Points Awarded				Total
1. Jacquie Allen	Wales	9·0	8·9	8·9	8·9	8·90
2. Mary Chamberlaine	England	9·3	9·3	9·5	9·4	9·35
3. Randall Bevan	Wales	9·4	9·3	9·0	9·6	9·35
4. Pat Winkle	England	9·3	9·2	8·9	9·7	9·25

The result was again a win for England:
ENGLAND 18·60   WALES 18·25

On 31st May 1963, five countries competed in a festival of gymnastics at a small town called Wageningen in Holland. The festival was called a Gymwa and it marked the 7th Centenary Celebrations of Wageningen. The five countries were the Netherlands, Germany, Switzerland, Belgium and England. We sent a trampoline team which competed in a five-way international. Our team consisted of Lila Webb, Chris Netherton, Joyce Thomas, David Smith, Yvonne Horne, Johnnie Ions and myself as team manager-cum-judge-cum-coach.

The Women's Team Competition was first. The countries competing were the Netherlands, Germany and England. Unfortunately Belgium and Switzerland could not raise a team for this match. The No. 1 woman from each country bounced first, followed by the second named and then the third. The final positions were as follows:

1st	W. Dibbett, Netherlands	18·60
2nd	E. Bagchus, Netherlands	18·45
3rd	Joyce Thomas, England	18·40
4th	Gisela Haferkamp, Germany	18·20
5th	Gisela Germar, Germany	18·10
6th	Lila Webb, England	18·00
7th	Yvonne Horne, England	17·90
8th	M. Ravesloot, Netherlands	17·80
9th	Gerda Schmidt, Germany	12·25

The competition was so close that only 0·10 of a point prevented us from getting all three of our competitors into the final. The Ladies team result was:

1st	Netherlands	54·85
2nd	England	54·30
3rd	Germany	48·55

Although it is somewhat frustrating to be so close and yet so far

166

from the Team Championship title, our hats were raised to the Dutch girls who bounced so consistently that this was the deciding factor.

Next, the Men's event. The order of bouncing was the same as for the women. This time there were five countries competing: the Netherlands, Belgium, Germany, England and Switzerland. We took the lead right from the start and all three of our men scored the highest marks on both the set and voluntary routines to give a finishing order of 1st, 2nd and 3rd. What a pleasant sight to see the complete English team lead the rest of Europe so confidently. Our boys certainly won the hearts of the crowd.

The individual positions for the Team event were:

1st	Chris Netherton, England	19·15
2nd	David Smith, England	19·00
3rd	Johnnie Ions, England	18·90
4th	Dieter Schulz, Germany	18·75
5th	Horst Schlindwein, Germany	18·55
6th	Hartmut Riehle, Germany	18·50
7th	Thomas Kaech, Switzerland	18·50
8th	Freddy Coppens, Belgium	18·20
9th	Ernst Morti, Switzerland	18·00
10th	Kurt Pauli, Switzerland	17·95
11th	W. Cleton, Netherlands	17·90
12th	A. Liebiecht, Belgium	17·80
13th	M. H. de Ruiter, Netherlands	17·75
14th	J. Mulder, Netherlands	15·70
15th	André Herman, Belgium	13·50

1st	England	57·05
2nd	Germany	55·80
3rd	Switzerland	54·45
4th	Netherlands	51·35
5th	Belgium	46·50

Saturday evening saw the finals of the Individual Competition. The first six competitors from the afternoon's placings went forward for this final. Lila bounced first to set the standard, but unfortunately, she did not bounce in her usual manner. Her final stunt, a double somie to seat, was short and each contact with the bed in getting to her feet was counted out. There was a total of four bounces too many and precious points were lost. Although very nervous during competition, Joyce Thomas always gave the appearance of absolute confidence. This, I feel, is where she had the edge over her competitors in such a close and tense final. Bouncing third, Joyce's points for her final routine were higher than the leading two competitors. Then Gisela Haferkamp, the German No. 1, who was hot on Joyce's heels, performed beautifully to score the highest points of the whole competition. Tension mounted. What a competition! Almost with a sigh of relief as the competition ended and tension relaxed, everyone got busy with pencil and paper. Joyce, biting her fingers, remarked, 'Third place seems to be my stumbling-block. I just cannot get any higher than third.' Just at this moment Gisela Haferkamp, the German girl, took a bewildered Joyce by the hand as she tried to explain, in a mixture of German and hand signals, her congratulations to Joyce on winning. Not knowing what to believe we all waited for the official result—'First, Joyce Thomas, England, 27·75.' I don't think Joyce knew whether to scream with delight or cry with happiness—in fact she was not the only one.

2nd	G. Haferkamp, Germany	27·70
3rd	E. Bagchus, Netherlands	27·70
4th	Gisela Germar, Germany	27·20
5th	Lila Webb, England	26·30
6th	W. Dibbet, Netherlands	25·90

Gisela Haferkamp was placed second over E. Bagchus because of a better set routine.

Now for the Men's Individual Competition. The excitement in our camp was overwhelming and I was only hoping that the tension would not spoil their performances. Bouncing with the cool confidence they possessed in the Team Competition, our boys performed superbly again, showing that they were undoubtedly the best team there.

The final result was:

1st	Chris Netherton, England	28·80
2nd	David Smith, England	28·45
3rd	Johnnie Ions, England	28·40
4th	Dieter Schulz, Germany	28·35
5th	Thomas Kaech, Switzerland	27·60
6th	Hartmut Riehle, Germany	27·10
7th	Horst Schlindwein, Germany	27·05

In July 1963, the top three trampolinists from the United States Gymnastic Federation, Danny Millman, George Hery and Fred Saunders made a tour of Germany, France and England demonstrating their skills and furthering the art of trampolining. In the October, Danny Millman won the now-established Fahrbach-Schuster Cup competition in Germany and returned to the United States with the title. Chris Netherton came fourth and Mary Chamberlaine of England won the Ladies' competition. It was this year that Poland held their First National Championships.

Throughout all this time there prevailed a great deal of anta-gonism between the B.A.G.A. Trampoline Committee and the splinter group known as the British Trampoline Association. The B.T.A. was highly organized and very soon flooded the country with propaganda concerning its various schemes. Many of the trampolinists revelled in this state of affairs since there were two coaching schemes, two proficiency award schemes, plenty of certificates to be obtained and twice as many competi-tions to enter.

On 19th November, a team of five girls travelled to Kiel in Germany together with Miss Eileen Cooper as team manager and Pete Quinney as judge. The competitors were Mary Cham-berlaine, Marilyn Clee, Joyce Cosgrave, Lila Webb and a young girl named Lynda Ball.

The first round of the competition consisted of the compul-sory and one voluntary routine. The voluntary routine was to be of a limited tariff of 6·00. This meant that if the degree of diffi-culty of the routine was higher than 6·00 no extra marks would be awarded. At the end of this round, Great Britain led in the competition by 72·45 marks to 71·80. Dr. Braecklein of Ger-many suggested that the final voluntary routine should be un-limited in its difficulty. After the introduction of the teams, Lynda Ball, our youngest competitor bounced first. As the youngest member, she performed very creditably under inter-national conditions.

The full results were:

Name	Country	Set	1st Vol.	2nd Vol.	Total	Position
Gerda Schmidt	W.G.	9·45	9·00	9·60	28·05	1
Mary Chamberlaine	G.B.	9·25	9·30	9·45	28·00	2
Helga Floehl	W.G.	9·30	9·10	9·35	27·75	3
Lila Webb	G.B.	9·30	8·70	9·10	27·10	4
Lynda Ball	G.B.	8·90	9·10	8·90	26·90	5
Gisela Germar	W.G.	9·10	8·50	9·25	26·85	6
Marilyn Clee	G.B.	9·05	8·60	9·15	26·80	7
Joyce Cosgrave	G.B.	9·05	8·85	8·85	26·75	8
Doris Stockman	W.G.	9·00	8·35	7·90	25·25	9
Maria Jarosch	W.G.	9·10	6·65	9·00	24·75	10

The National Championships seemed to get earlier and earlier in the year. The preliminary rounds for the 1964 Championships at De Montfort Hall, Leicester, were held on 14th December 1963—a similar circumstance to last year when the preliminary competitions were held at the end of the previous year. Great importance was placed on the championships that year because of the pending international matches. Every competitor wanted to put on a good show in order to be considered for international honours.

The finals of the Men's and Ladies' competitions took place on 15th February 1964 at the Royal Albert Hall.

NATIONAL TRAMPOLINE CHAMPIONSHIPS, 1964
BOYS

Name	Preliminary	Final (Vol. only)	Total	Position
Curtis	18·40	9·45	27·85	1
Maddy	18·35	9·25	27·60	2
Melhearne	17·70	9·10	26·80	3
Tinsley	17·85	7·65	25·50	4
Harris	17·15	7·20	24·35	5

GIRLS

Name	Preliminary	Final (Vol. only)	Total	Position
Sue Vine	18·40	9·20	27·60	1
M. Ratcliffe	18·35	9·20	27·55	2
A. Goddard	18·30	9·00	27·30	3
Barbara John	17·45	9·05	26·50	4
Gill Walder	17·40	8·50	25·90	5

HISTORY

LADIES

Name	Preliminary	Set	Vol.	Total	Position
Mary Hunkin (*née* Chamberlaine)	18·80	9·10	9·25	37·15	1
Lynda Ball	18·60	9·05	9·25	36·90	2
Marilyn Clee	18·40	9·25	9·20	36·85	3
Joyce Cosgrave (*née* Thomas)	18·50	9·15	8·15	35·80	4
Sheila Hawtin	17·95	9·00	8·85	35·80	5

Joyce Cosgrave was given fourth place over Sheila Hawtin because of a higher mark in the preliminary round.

MEN

Name	Preliminary	Set	Vol.	Total	Position
Chris Netherton	18·70	9·40	9·20	37·30	1
Alex Howden	18·20	9·30	9·30	36·80	2
David Lease	18·25	9·30	9·00	36·55	3
Johnny Ions	18·00	9·10	9·15	36·25	4
Mike Williams	17·90	9·00	—	26·90	5

In the early part of March 1964, the United States Gymnastic Federation's trampoline team consisting of Frank Schmitz, Steve Johnson and Nancy Smith, toured South Africa for six weeks. The tour was most successful with the men taking first and second places and Nancy first place in the South African Championship.

The biggest step forward in the history of trampolining was taken when England staged the first ever World Trampoline Championships on the 21st March 1964 at the Royal Albert Hall. The whole competition was the brainwave of Ted Blake and was presented by Nissen Trampoline Co. Ltd. in conjunction with the British Amateur Gymnastic Association's Trampoline Committee. Never before were so many international competitors brought together to pit their skill for the most coveted title of any sportsman—'The Champion of the World'. Competitors represented twelve different countries—two men and two women competitors were allowed to compete from each country. The only exception was the U.S.A. where two organizations govern trampolining; The Amateur Athletic Union and the U.S. Gymnastic Federation. For this reason there were four competitors from U.S.A. The countries represented were Belgium, Denmark, England, Holland, Norway, Scotland, South Africa, Sweden, Switzerland, U.S.A., Wales and West Germany.

What an occasion! Every top name in trampolining was there from the spheres of both the competitors and officials. The names are too many to list here but even today these names are still world-renowned. Because so many countries took part and each had its own rules and regulations, it was decided to run the competitions on a knock-out basis. Each judge, using the rules of his own country, only had to decide which of two competitors was the better. The rules, therefore, were simple:

1. The competitions were for individual honours—no team contest.
2. The competitors were matched against each other in pairs and competed in a double elimination, knock-out tournament.
3. Working on the knowledge of each competitor's standard, the performers were seeded so that the better ones would not meet each other until the closing stages. A draw was made for byes and the order of performance between competing pairs.
4. The winners in each round advanced through succeeding rounds to the final. Losers in the *first* round were allowed a place in a separate losers' consolation tournament.
5. An assessment panel consisting of seven international judges was chosen, one from each of the competing countries. The judges only had to decide which competitor was the winner of each competing pair.
6. Each competitor had to present one optional ten-bounce routine. No second attempts were allowed.

The draw and results were as on pages 174 and 175.

To prove to everyone that trampolining did not kill natural spring and that this sport could be used as a carry-over to other sports, the two champions performed routines on the ground. Young Judy Wills thrilled everyone with her consecutive hollow back somersaults with a few full twisters and double twisters thrown in for good measure. Then Danny Millman left everyone simply amazed by performing a double backward somersault on the ground, a feat which could only be accomplished by a selected few. London had never seen anything like this before.

On the day after the World Championships, a meeting was held for all the delegates from the different countries with a view to setting up an International Trampoline Federation. This meeting, again the brain-wave of Ted Blake, was held at St. Mary's College, Twickenham, on Sunday, 22nd March 1964. With so many representatives from different countries together for the first time, it seemed only natural to meet together and discuss the future of trampolining in the world.

Those present included:

England	B.A.G.A.	Mr. D. Taylor
England	B.T.A.	Mr. G. S. Aaron
U.S.A.	A.A.U.	Mr. J. Hennessy
U.S.A.	U.S.G.F.	Dr. N. Loken
Holland	K.N.G.V.	Dr. O. J. Gerritsen
Norway	N.S.F.	Mr. G. Vegard
Switzerland	E.T.V.	Mr. K. Baechler
Denmark		Mrs. S. Kraemer
Sweden		Mr. S. Carlsson
Germany	D.T.B.	Dr. H. Braecklein
Belgium		Mr. Croonenborghs representing the trampolinine commission of the Fédération Royale Belge de Gymnastique and the trampoline commission of the university.

Every delegate representing his country's organization voted that the International Federation of Trampolining should be formulated. So once more another great stride was taken in the progress of trampolining.

A resolution was passed that each country should send a representative to a meeting to be held in four months' time in Frankfurt. At this meeting the following people were elected to hold office for one year.

173

FIRST WORLD'S OPEN TRAMPOLINE CHAMPIONSHIPS
Saturday, 21st March 1964
Draw for Men's Competition

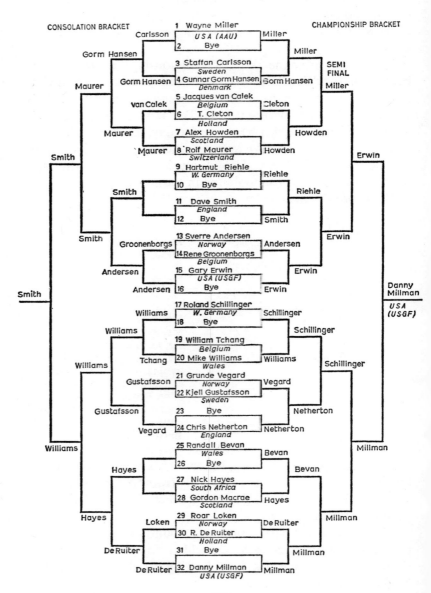

174

FIRST WORLD'S OPEN TRAMPOLINE CHAMPIONSHIPS
Saturday, 21st March 1964
Draw for Ladies' Competition

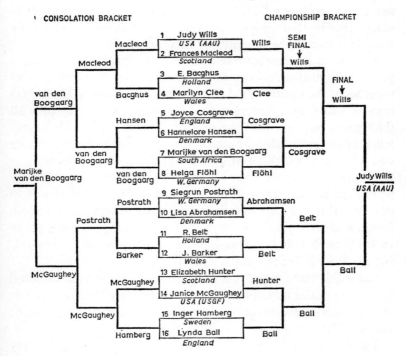

René Schaerer	Switzerland	President
Ted Blake, B.T.F.	Great Britain	Vice President
Erich Kinzel, D.T.B.	W. Germany	General Secretary
Richard Vereecken, F.R.B.G.	Belgium	Treasurer

Bob Bollinger of the U.S.G.F. distributed news of his Axial Rotation method of marking. He felt very strongly and sincerely that this was the only fair way to judge trampoline competitions. For his work in this field, Bob was awarded the McCloy Research Award in the U.S.A. It certainly does give credit to difficulty, leaving the judges to mark for style only. The only trouble is that at the present it is slightly involved.

That same evening representatives from the B.A.G.A. Trampoline Committee and the British Trampoline Association met together at the Central Y.M.C.A. in London, again at the invitation of Ted Blake. The idea of this meeting was to resolve all differences between the two parties. By combining the knowledge of the men behind both powers, this collective experience could be used in making Britain one of the leading authorities in the world of trampolining. The members of both councils were somewhat wary of each others' motives at first, but it was soon discovered that everyone was relieved by the suggestion to join forces and welcomed the merger. The new marriage was to be called 'The British Amateur Gymnastic Association incorporating the British Trampoline Association'.

Later this same month on the 28th and 30th, we were offered an international match against West Germany to take place at the Empire Pool, Wembley, on the occasion of the A.A.A. Indoor Championships.

The competition ran over the two days of Easter Saturday and Easter Monday. At the finish of the last event before the interval, the whole arena was thrown into total darkness. Then at one end of the stadium the beam of a searchlight lit up the two teams as they marched to the centre of the arena. It was touches like this that did much to present our sport to the public in an exciting manner.

The result of the match was calculated to include the four highest scorers only on each day.

176

GREAT BRITAIN

Competitor	Saturday	Monday	Total
Dave Smith	32·20	32·25	64·45
Chris Netherton	32·30	31·95	64·25
Mike Williams	31·95	31·75	63·70
John Newton	31·50	30·80	62·30
Alex Howden	20·60	32·20	52·80
Team total	127·95	128·15	256·10

WEST GERMANY

Competitor	Saturday	Monday	Total
Michael Budenberg	31·85	32·45	64·75
Werner Willig	31·55	32·40	63·95
Harmutt Reihle	31·35	32·50	63·85
Horst Schlindwein	31·85	31·05	62·90
Manfred Haase	31·60	30·60	62·20
Team total	126·85	128·40	255·25

Each country won one round with Great Britain winning overall by 0·85. On Saturday evening the challenge went up that Germany would take on England at Ten-pin Bowling. After some unusual bowling England emerged the winners by 583 to 426.

On 25th April 1964, Staff Sergeant Johnnie Ions of the Army Gymnastic Union visited Brussels to see the Belgium Trampoline Championships. Although the competition was a closed event Johnnie was somehow persuaded to compete. As an ex-member of the English team he showed everyone that he was still no mean performer. The results were as follows:

Name	Set	1st Vol.	2nd Vol.	Total	Position
J. Ions (Great Britain)	9·45	9·80	9·80	29·05	1
F. Coppens (Drongen)	8·95	9·35	9·35	27·65	2
W. Tchang (Brussels)	9·05	8·15	8·90	26·10	3
V. Stynne (Louvain)	8·90	8·05	8·30	25·25	4
A. Van De Voorde (Halle)	8·00	8·60	8·15	24·75	5

Although Johnnie Ions was placed first he could not be

awarded the Belgian title as this had to go to a Belgian. However, he was honoured instead with the *Hors Concours*.

To follow up this achievement on the Continent, a group of English bouncers teamed together and travelled to Burstadt in West Germany for a 12-Nation International Invitation Competition on Saturday, 16th May 1964. The team consisted of Joyce Cosgrave, Chris Netherton, Johnnie Newton, Johnnie Ions and Les Mirasole. The competition started in the afternoon with the set exercises. Werner Willig of Germany was in the lead with Chris Netherton second, Johnnie Newton and Johnnie Ions third and fourth. Then came the voluntary routines and all four of the English boys got through to the final five. No scores were shown, only places, and it was very difficult to see just what the judges wanted. In the second round of voluntary routines John Newton really excelled himself with a first-class performance to take first place, overhauling Werner Willig and Chris Netherton. The final placings were:

1st	Newton
2nd	Willig
3rd	Netherton
4th	Ions
5th	Mirasole

Les Mirasole performed very well in his very first international to take fifth place.

In the Ladies' competition Joyce Cosgrave was in a class of her own to take first place. It was unfortunate that none of the better-class German ladies was competing to make the competition more interesting.

During the past eighteen months, British trampolinists had certainly made their presence felt on the Continent. Mary Chamberlaine, Joyce Cosgrave, Johnnie Ions, Chris Netherton, John Newton and Pat Winkle all took senior European titles during various visits.

It is recorded earlier in this book that the Kent County Schools Rebound Tumbling Association came into being in March 1961. Almost three years later to the month Essex County, which was the home of trampolining, was the second to set up its own Schools' Association. Their first championships were held at Belfairs High Schools, Leigh-on-Sea, on 25th April 1964.

During all these years from when England first imported the trampoline until now, the sport which was of American origin had swept right across the Continent, Europe, Scandinavia, Africa and now into the Far East and Russia. Australia held their first National Championships in Sydney in August 1964, and Russia's first National Championships were held on 14th–17th October in Erevan. The result of this latter competition was:

1st	Viktor Palagin	TsSKA (Central Army Sports Board)
2nd	Yuri Melnikov	TsSKA (Central Army Sports Board)
3rd	Valery Gorbunov	'Burevestnik', Orenburg

Here again we have a new country in its first competition using a ten-bounce routine system. Each competitor had to perform two compulsory routines and one optional. The difficulty-rating in their routines could already hold their own against many of the top countries at this time but they made it even more difficult for themselves by using bad combinations. For example, Viktor Palagin's winning routine was:

1. Double back somersault.
2. Rudolph.
3. Back somersault.
4. Barani-out fliffus.
5. Forward somersault with full-twist.
6. Back somersault with full-twist.
7. Back somersault with one and a half twist.
8. Back somersault.
9. Back one and three-quarter somersault.
10. Full twisting Cody.

Valery Gorbunov who came third used similar changes of direction:

1. Back somersault with double-twist.
2. Forward one and a quarter somersault.
3. Back Cody.
4. Back somersault with full-twist.
5. Barani.
6. Forward somersault (tucked).
7. Forward somersault with full-twist.
8. Straddle Jump.
9. Double forward somersault.
10. Double back somersault.

179

It was also on 11th November 1964 that Japan held its first National Championships at Osaka City Gymnasium. Because the Gymnastic Federation in Japan has a minimum age limit of 18 years, the entries were restricted to thirteen men and seven women. The results were as follows:

WOMEN			MEN		
1st	M. Omote	9·00	1st	C. Kato	9·50
2nd	Y. Noda	8·70	2nd	R. Ogata	9·45
3rd	K. Murakami	8·60	3rd	T. Hasegawa	9·40

The competition was held on a $1\frac{3}{4}$ in. web bed. Kato's winning routine was:

1. Back somersault with full-twist.
2. Layout back.
3. Double backward somersault.
4. Back somersault with double-twist.
5. Back somersault.
6. One and three-quarter forward somersaults with half-twist to stomach.
7. Back Cody.
8. Back somersault with double-twist.
9. Back somersault.
10. Double back somersault.

Considering that this was their first contest and a ten-bounce routine had to be performed, a very high standard was achieved. Ryogo Ogata who came second in this competition, you will see later was Japan's representative at the 1966 World Championships.

The preliminary competitions for the 1965 National Championships were held on 28th November 1964 in Leicester once more. The results were as follows:

BOYS

Name	Preliminary	Final	Position
M. McCarthy	17·75	27·30	1
G. Maddy	17·60	27·15	2
P. Mulhearne	17·30	26·50	3
R. Hughes	17·10	26·50	4
S. Harris	16·75	25·55	5

GIRLS

Name	Preliminary	Final	Position
B. John	18·75	28·05	1
A. Goddard	18·30	27·65	2
M. Ratcliffe	17·95	27·15	3
J. Hooper	17·00	25·75	4
J. Bradley	16·80	25·25	5

The Men's and Women's finals were held at the Royal Albert Hall as usual. It was five years since we had first had the honour to present the finals of the Senior Championships in this great hall and those were five very important years. During this time, trampolining received a great boost in one way or another. The great names who provided the excitement in those days have passed from the competitive scene—names like Mary Chamberlaine, Randall Bevan and Pat Winkle. Only Dave Smith continued the fight but times had to change and now young blood and new names have taken over. It is interesting to note the names of two of the finalists in the Junior Championships in 1961. A young girl of 13 by the name of Lynda Ball took fourth position and 15-year-old Mike Williams tied for first place in the Boys' competition.

The finals which took place on 23rd January 1965, proved to be the farewell presentation of trampolining with the B.A.G.A. in this arena. Once again another chapter in the history of trampolining was closed as further progress had to be made.

NATIONAL TRAMPOLINING CHAMPIONSHIP, 1965

LADIES

Name	Preliminary	Final	Total	Position
Lynda Ball	18·00	9·50	27·50	1
Barbara John	17·65	9·20	26·85	2
Anne Goddard	17·05	8·70	25·75	3
Sue Vine	17·00	8·70	25·70	4
Margaret Badgery	16·95	8·75	25·70	5

Sue Vine was awarded fourth place over Margaret Badgery because of a better preliminary mark.

181

MEN

Name	Preliminary	Final	Total	Position
Chris Netherton	18·85	9·45	28·30	1
Mike Williams	18·90	9·40	28·30	2
Dave Curtis	18·80	9·40	28·20	3
Dave Smith	18·75	9·00	27·75	4
John Newton	18·30	9·10	27·40	5

Chris Netherton was acclaimed the new British Champion because of a higher mark received for his compulsory routine.

The Staffordshire Schools' Association was formed during this year.

The timing of our National Championship Final fitted in nicely with the dates for the Second World Championships. Once again, we in England had the honour of staging these World Championships at the Royal Albert Hall. The date was 30th January 1965.

That year twelve different countries entered but only eleven competed as the Belgium team had to withdraw. Two others, Holland and Switzerland, which entered the first year did not compete in this second championship. However, two new countries sent entries, the Lebanon and Australia. The Australian representative, Don Viney, later met with misfortune in 1966. The biggest surprise of all was the defeat of the reigning world champion Danny Millman in the trials. Everyone was disappointed that he would be unable to defend his title on this great occasion.

The competitions were again marked on the knock-out system but the seeding was arranged by using the Axial Rotation system mentioned earlier, and three further championships were added to the programme, the synchronized Team Competition and the Men's and Women's Tumbling Championships. It is interesting to note that of the thirteen entries for the tumbling, eight of them were trampolinists. The three competitors in the Ladies' section were all trampolinists and of the four semi-finalists in the Men's section, two were trampolinists, one being the ultimate winner.

182

HISTORY

SECOND WORLD OPEN TRAMPOLINE CHAMPIONSHIPS

The draw and results were as on pages 184 and 185.

FIRST WORLD OPEN TUMBLING CHAMPIONSHIPS

The draw and results were as on page 186.

The championships again gave delegates of the International Trampoline Federation an opportunity to meet together to discuss the promotion of the sport. Among the important items discussed, one was that the U.S.A. should have more than one vote since they have two associations and also far more assistance to offer the sport. The reply was that it was an American problem which should be resolved by them, and that the two associations should co-operate and merge into one group. Great Britain was in a similar position with the B.A.G.A. Trampoline Committee and the B.T.A.! Another item was that the Federation should try to get trampolining acknowledged as an Olympic sport. But the most important item of all was that the technical committee should prepare a set of international rules to be used universally.

The next big international match in England was a combined gymnastics and trampoline competition against the U.S.A., held at Wembley Sports Arena on 20th March 1965. This was really an opportunity to show the British public some top gymnasts from abroad, rather than being a closely fought contest. Like all the British Championship finals which were held at the Royal Albert Hall, the *Sun* newspaper presented the meeting in conjunction with the B.A.G.A. Only one man and one woman represented each country. For Great Britain they were Lynda Ball and Mike Williams and for the U.S.A., Beverly Averyt and Keen Day. The Americans have such a depth of top performers in Men's trampolining that nearly every time we meet there is a new face to be seen. Each performer executed two voluntary routines and the results of the two competitions decided the winners. The results were as follows:

Second World's Open Trampolining Championships
Saturday, 30th January 1965
Draw for Men's Competition

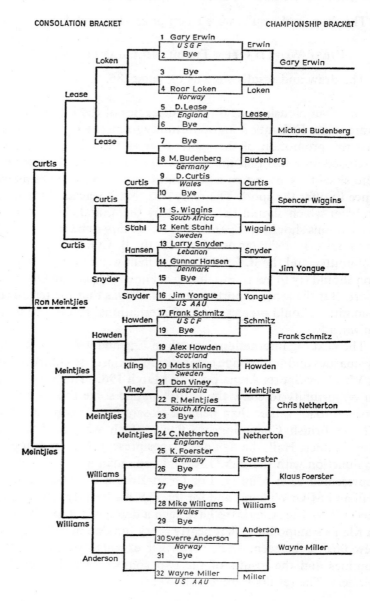

CONSOLATION BRACKET

CHAMPIONSHIP BRACKET

184

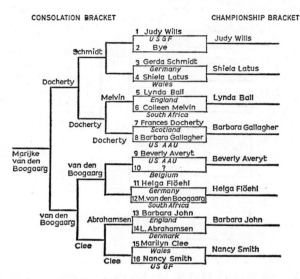

CONSOLATION BRACKET   CHAMPIONSHIP BRACKET

Men's 'A' Class Trampoline Final Bracket

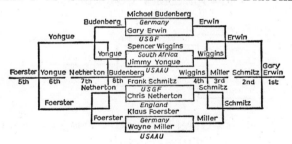

Ladies' 'A' Class Trampoline Final Bracket

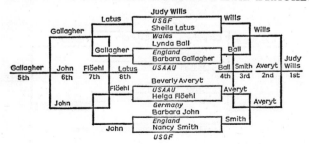

185

First World's Open Tumbling Championships
Draw for Men's Competition

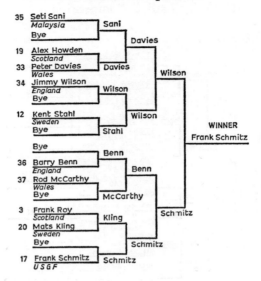

```
35  Seti Sani
    Malaysia          Sani
    Bye                          Davies
19  Alex Howden
    Scotland
33  Peter Davies      Davies
    Wales                        Wilson
34  Jimmy Wilson
    England           Wilson
    Bye
12  Kent Stahl                   Wilson
    Sweden
    Bye               Stahl                    WINNER
                                               Frank Schmitz
    Bye               Benn
36  Barry Benn
    England                      Benn
37  Rod McCarthy
    Wales
    Bye               McCarthy
 3  Frank Roy                                 Schmitz
    Scotland          Kling
20  Mats Kling
    Sweden
    Bye                          Schmitz
17  Frank Schmitz     Schmitz
    USGF
```

First World's Open Tumbling Championships
Draw for Ladies' Competition

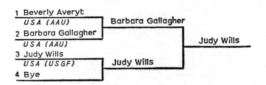

```
1 Beverly Averyt
  USA (AAU)          Barbara Gallagher
2 Barbara Gallagher
  USA (AAU)                               Judy Wills
3 Judy Wills
  USA (USGF)         Judy Wills
4 Bye
```

First World's Open Synchronized Trampoline
Championships
Draw for Team Competition

```
                        USGF
            ENGLAND  Gary Erwin, Frank Schmitz  USGF
                        ENGLAND
                     Lynda Ball  Barbara John
ENGLAND                                                USGF
                        WEST GERMANY
        SOUTH AFRICA  Michael Budenberg, Helga Flöehl  WEST GERMANY
                        SOUTH AFRICA
            Marijke van den Boogaarg, Colleen Melvin
```

186

LADIES

		1st Vol.	2nd Vol.	Total
Lynda Ball	G.B.	9·05	9·05	18·10
Beverly Averyt	U.S.A.	9·30	9·35	18·65

MEN

		1st Vol.	2nd Vol.	Total
Michael Williams	G.B.	8·10	9·20	17·30
Keen Day	U.S.A.	9·20	9·10	18·30

Result: U.S.A. 36·95   G.B. 35·40

Had Mike not been unsure of his first routine the result would have been very, very close. Afterwards the teams and officials were given a reception in a London hotel and so a most enjoyable time was had by all. Many new friends were made and the established ones reunited.

1965 saw the formation of the English Schools' Association, and their first National Championships were held at the Assembly Hall in Barking, Essex, on 12th June. Competitors travelled from as far as Lincolnshire, Staffordshire, Warwickshire, Bristol, Somerset and from Kent, London and Essex. This was a most successful venture and a useful stepping-stone for competitors aiming for international honours. Competing at this championship were two performers who had represented England in the last World Championships, Barbara John and Lynda Ball. Lynda, of course, is our most experienced international competitor. There was also a young lad under 15 years of age by the name of Kilford who later, in 1966, represented England in a friendly match against Wales.

The following day, 13th June 1965, the trampoline committees of the B.A.G.A. and the B.T.A. finally came to an amicable arrangement after two and a half years of fighting each other. The two associations agreed to pool all their resources and join together to form the British Trampoline Federation Ltd. The historic occasion of the signing of the Articles of Association took place in the meeting room of the Central Council of Physical Recreation in London on Sunday, 10th October at 2.30

p.m. and was officially incorporated on 1st November 1965. Trampolining in Britain was united once more under one governing body. This pact immediately cleared up the many problems which would have been evident in international trampolining. The U.S.A. still has a greater problem, but in time, who knows, even they may produce one Association responsible for trampolining in America.

At a meeting of the International Trampoline Federation in Basle, Switzerland, on the 31st July, the main officers of the Presidium were re-elected. At the same meeting a technical committee was formed to work on a new set of international rules. The committee consists of:

Dr. Heinz Braecklein D.T.B. (W. Germany) President of the technical committee
Kurt Baechler E.T.V. (Switzerland)
Klass Boot (Holland)
Jeff Hennessy A.A.U. (U.S.A.)
Pat Winkle B.T.F. (Great Britain)

This year also saw the formation of the French Trampoline Federation.

President — Christian Ledoux
Vice-President, Gen. Sec. — André Pottier
2nd Vice-President — Bernard Ammon
Assist. Gen. Secretary — Bernard Courtoison
Treasurer — René Cagny
Assist. Treasurer — Bernard Burger

BRITISH TOUR TO THE REPUBLIC OF SOUTH AFRICA, 1965

BRITISH TEAM
Manager: Dennis Taylor
Coach: John Ley
Girls: Lynda Ball
Barbara John
Men: Mike Williams
David Curtis

SOUTH AFRICAN TEAM
Manager: 'Jannie' Jansen
Coach: Tommy Steyn
Girls: Chantal Fouche
Susan Warne
Men: Ronnie Meintjies
Spencer Wiggins

The matches were keenly fought on each occasion and all performers gave good accounts of themselves. The British men and women trained quite hard and certainly poured on the difficulty in their routines throughout the tour.

Results

1. NATAL MATCH

1st	S. Warne (N)	17·45	2nd	L. Ball (B)	17·40
3rd	B. John (B)	14·20			

Total for Great Britain 31·60   *Total for Natal* 33·80

1. 1ST TEST MATCH

1st	B. John (B)	17·80	2nd	Lynda Ball (B)	17·80
3rd	S. Warne (S.A.)	17·60	4th	C. Fouche (S.A.)	17·50

Total for Great Britain 35·60   *Total for South Africa* 35·10

3. 2ND TEST MATCH (Men)

1st	S. Wiggins (S.A.)	9.35	2nd	R. Meintjies (S.A.)	9·25
3rd	M. Williams (B)	9·20	4th	D. Curtis (B)	9·15

Total for Great Britain 36·40   *Total for South Africa* 37·40

4. TRANSVAAL MATCH (Women)   (Men)

1. Lynda Ball	9·05	1. Ronnie Meintjies	8·95
2. Barbara John	8·70	2. Spencer Wiggins	9·20
3. Colleen Melvin	8·75	3. Breedt	8·65
4. Piev Aieborn	8·80	4. Peter Melvin	8·95
5. Jennifer Liebenberg	8·60	5. Mike Williams	9·10
6. Pam Melvin	8·05	6. Dave Curtis	9·00
		7. Dirk Odendaal	8·45

1st	Lynda Ball	9·05	1st	Spencer Wiggins	9·20
2nd	Piev Aieborn	8·80	2nd	Mike Williams	9·10
3rd	Colleen Melvin	8·75	3rd	Dave Curtis	9·00

The first National Championships of the British Trampoline Federation were held on Saturday, 5th March 1966, in the Fox Gymnasium of the Army School of P.T., Aldershot. This was the first time that the National Trampoline competitions were held on their own. The complete championships took place on the same day, including the finals of the Men's and Women's contest and the trials for the Third World Championships. A separate trial had to be held for the World Championships because on this occasion the new international rules were to be used. These new rules could make all the difference to the result of the competition as held under the old British rules and, therefore, the result of the National Championships could not be used to select the World Championships team.

189

HISTORY

This year, the competitors had the choice of performing on either a 1-in. or ½-in. web bed. Some of the bouncers chose the ½-in. web because it was better but unfortunately they were not used to controlling its reaction. The reigning British champion, Chris Netherton, was one of these and he finished in fifteenth position.

The results were:

GIRLS

Name	Set	Vol.	Final	Total	Position
Gill Walder	9·00	8·85	8·95	26·80	1
Wendy Coulton	8·55	8·95	9·25	26·75	2
Anne Sloan	8·45	8·15	8·60	25·20	3
Janet Hooper	7·95	8·55	8·70	25·20	4
Linda Bevis	8·15	8·25	8·45	24·85	5

BOYS

Name	Set	Vol.	Final	Total	Position
D. Kilford	8·90	9·25	9·00	27·15	1
R. Hughes	8·60	8·95	9·00	26·55	2
W. Atkin	8·50	8·50	8·35	25·35	3
A. Hughes	8·45	8·35	6·00	22·80	4
S. Jay	8·25	8·45	6·00	22·70	5

LADIES

Name	Set	Vol.	Final	Total	Position
Lynda Ball	8·70	9·50	9·50	27·70	1
Barbara John	8·90	9·05	9·15	27·10	2
Gill Walder	8·40	8·60	8·80	25·80	3
Sue Vine	8·45	8·85	8·45	25·75	4
M. Ratcliffe	8·10	8·50	8·45	25·05	5

MEN

Name	Set	Vol.	Final	Total	Position
Dave Curtis	9·00	9·40	9·35	27·75	1
Mike Williams	9·00	9·45	9·25	27·70	2
Clive Brigden	8·55	8·65	8·80	26·00	3
Derek Kilford	8·60	8·75	8·45	25·80	4
John Newton	8·65	8·80	7·55	25·00	5

The results of the trial for the World Championships were:

> 1st   Lynda Ball
> 2nd   Wendy Coulton
> (In the National Championships,
> Wendy could only place 8th)

> 1st   Dave Curtis
> 2nd   Clive Brigden

Prior to going to America for the Third World Championships, the T.W.W. television network in Wales gave us the opportunity of staging an England versus Wales international competition on 12th April. Each team was to consist of four men who would perform one compulsory routine and two voluntary routines. It seemed to be the wrong time for some of the competitors. The National Championships were finished and the team to represent Great Britain at the World Championships had been selected. The climax had been reached and the pressure was off. Competitors were relaxing and seemed unprepared for another big competition. With the exception of Dave Curtis, who usually seemed to hold his form, the big names had an off-day. Two of the leading juniors, Robert Hughes and Derek Kilford, were selected to represent England on this occasion in order to give them high-class competition experience in preparation for the future. These two boys soon showed that they were already well prepared for full-scale international competition by beating all the other competitors excepting Dave Curtis.

The result was as follows:

Name		Set	1st Vol.	2nd Vol.	Total	Position
Dave Curtis	(W)	9·25	9·25	8·85	27·35	1
Robert Hughes	(E)	8·85	8·80	9·25	26·90	2
Derek Kilford	(E)	8·95	8·65	9·00	26·60	3
John Newton	(E)	8·80	8·80	8·85	26·45	4
Clive Brigden	(E)	8·75	8·65	8·95	26·35	5
Glyn Maddy	(W)	8·65	8·30	8·60	25·55	6
Mike Williams	(W)	9·50	7·45	5·10	22·05	7
Malcolm Humphreys	(W)	8·95	4·20	8·10	21·25	8

Result: ENGLAND 106·30   WALES 96·20

The time began to draw near to the greatest day in our trampolining history—the World Championships being held in

America, the Mother Country of this wonderful sport. In the past we had only witnessed the ability of the American performers through the small teams which visited Britain on the occasion of top international competitions. Now we were to live amongst them and see them on their home ground. We were going to train with them, learn something of their methods and see for ourselves the depth of talent in the country. Before we could take on this journey, however, there was the enormous task of raising sufficient money to pay for all the costs involved. It was estimated that we had to raise £1,050 before we could send our team.

A great deal of effort was put into trying to obtain this amount and it was only in the actual week of leaving for the States that the total was realized. When the A.A.U. heard of our plight they immediately sent us two tickets so that should all our efforts have failed we would still have been able to send our best man and best woman. Representing us in the Ladies' Championships were two Bristol schoolgirls, Lynda Ball and Wendy Coulton. To make certain that they would both travel, their coach, John Ley, managed to get the Bristol Education Authority to donate £186 towards the girls' fare. This was followed by a donation of £130 from the Brook School, Loughton, Essex, who organized every conceivable money-raising fund in order to send Clive Brigden who was their representative for the team. Luckily Dave Curtis and I were able to use the two tickets sent to us by the A.A.U. £37 was raised from individual donations and collections and finally, on the very eve of our proposed flight, the Sports Council gave us a grant of £340 for overseas international competition. This was just the amount we needed; a truly eleventh-hour deliverance.

The British team consisted of four competitors, Lynda Ball, Wendy Coulton, Dave Curtis and Clive Brigden, and myself as team manager-cum-coach-cum-judge. We would have been unable to travel to the World Championships had it not been for the wonderful support given by all those people who contributed in some way or another to this cause. This assistance was greatly appreciated by each member of the team and whilst at the championships they did all they could to give of their best in return.

The competitors travelled to America from all parts of the globe; from the Continent, Europe, and as far east as Japan in one direction and from Australia in the south to Canada in the north.

Louisiana is the home of most of the top trampolinists in the U.S.A. and so it was the obvious choice for the venue. The humidity in Louisiana was very high, approximately 95°, and this was the first opponent with which we had to contend. Performing in such a temperature sapped the strength from our team so we had to spend time becoming acclimatized. A week or so before we left London, on 26th April, England had snow! The other countries had arrived a week to ten days before we did and so they were beginning to get used to it all. Competitors from South Africa and Australia felt that it was like home from home.

On Friday the 29th April the first of the four competitions (the Men's Synchronized event), took place in Blackham Coliseum, Lafayette. The competition consisted of the two male members from each team executing a swingtime routine of ten consecutive stunts at the same time on different trampolines. Marks were awarded for difficulty and precise timing.

Our two competitors bounced extremely well but unfortunately, on the very last movement, one of our performers 'lost' himself in the air and failed to execute his final stunt. Before this it had seemed that we were all set to capture the first title.

The final positions were:

1. U.S.A.   15·10
2. South Africa   13·45
3. Germany   12·75
4. Canada   12·05
5. GREAT BRITAIN   11·95

Even after the calamity of receiving lower marks than anticipated, we were still only 0·80 behind the Germans in third place.

The Ladies' Synchronized Championship was next. It was a foregone conclusion as to which team would win. The U.S.A. team consisted of two performers who finished first and second in the individual competition. Their marks for the synchronized event reached as high as 9·9 out of a possible 10·0. To this mark was added a difficulty-rating equal to that of the top men performers. The fight for second place was most exciting but again we just failed to make third place; this time by 0·40 of a mark.

1.	U.S.A.	14·90
2.	Germany	13·05
3.	South Africa	12·40
4.	GREAT BRITAIN	12·00

The next day (Saturday, 30th) the Individual Championships took place beginning with the Men's competition. This proved to be the most disappointing event of all for Britain. Our British champion, Dave Curtis, of whom we had great hopes, touched the suspension system during his routine and this terminated his performance. Even the Americans openly declared that Dave would be their nearest rival but, as so often happens in this unpredictable sport, it was the turn of another giant to tumble. The two Americans were fighting it out in the preliminary round to prove who was the better bouncer.

Wayne Miller scored 27·95 while Dave Jacobs scored 27·85. It was so close that all the stops had to be pulled out if a conclusive champion was to be found. Dave Jacobs took the gamble in a bid to overtake his rival and his final routine consisted of the following ten movements.

1. Triple backward somersault.
2. Double forward somersault with one and a half twists.
3. Double backward somersault.
4. Double forward somersault piked with half-twist.
5. Double backward somersault.
6. One and a half twisting forward somersault.
7. Backward somersault with full-twist.
8. Double backward somersault with full-twist.
9. Double backward somersault.
10. Triple backward somersault.

Unfortunately he 'lost' himself half-way through and was penalized for not performing his intended routine. Although Clive Brigden of Great Britain improved his performance to finish in eighth place in the final round, his two sets of marks for the preliminary and final rounds added together kept him in tenth place. The first ten performers only competed in the finals.

FINAL RESULTS

1.	Wayne Miller	U.S.A.	46·70
2.	Spencer Wiggins	South Africa	43·80
3.	Michael Budenberg	Germany	43·70
4.	Ian McNaughton	South Africa	43·55
5.	David Jacobs	U.S.A.	42·70
6.	Billy Popiwenko	Australia	40·20
7.	Dieter Schulz	Germany	40·05
8.	Rick Kinsman	Canada	39·60
9.	Wayne King	Canada	37·55
10.	CLIVE BRIGDEN	GREAT BRITAIN	36·80

14. DAVE CURTIS   GREAT BRITAIN
(Did not qualify for the final)

Throughout the preliminary round of the Ladies' Individual Championship, Lynda Ball of Great Britain maintained third position only 1·15 points behind the two Americans, but was edged out of this position in the final by 0·10 of a mark.

FINAL RESULT

1.	Judy Wills	U.S.A.	43·15
2.	Nancy Smith	U.S.A.	42·10
3.	Susan Warne	South Africa	39·65
4.	LYNDA BALL	GREAT BRITAIN	39·55
5.	Helga Flohe	Germany	38·90
6.	Maria Jarosch	Germany	38·15
7.	Charlene Paletz	South Africa	37·50
8.	WENDY COULTON	GREAT BRITAIN	37·45

Whilst in America all the countries were invited to enter for the A.A.U. National Championships which took place the weekend following the World Championships. In this competition only the first six competitors in the preliminary round went forward for the final.

LADIES' RESULT

1.	Judy Wills	U.S.A.	28·45
2.	Nancy Smith	U.S.A.	27·45
3.	Charlene Paletz	South Africa	25·30
4.	Susan Warne	South Africa	25·20
5.	LYNDA BALL	GREAT BRITAIN	23·95
6.	Judy Ann Ford	U.S.A.	21·05

7. WENDY COULTON   GREAT BRITAIN

MEN'S RESULT

1. Wayne Miller	U.S.A.	28·95
2. Dave Jacobs	U.S.A.	28·40
3. Jim Yongue	U.S.A.	27·90
4. Spencer Wiggins	South Africa	27·50
5. Ian McNaughton	South Africa	27·50
6. DAVE CURTIS	GREAT BRITAIN	26·70

14. CLIVE BRIGDEN	GREAT BRITAIN

Our overall results in these two major championships were:

WORLD CHAMPIONSHIPS	A.A.U. CHAMPIONSHIPS
2 × 4th positions	1 × 5th position
1 × 5th position	1 × 6th position
1 × 8th position	1 × 7th position
1 × 10th position	1 × 14th position
1 × 14th position	

We also made the finals in every competition and returned home with three trophies.

In May 1966, the Federation of Acrobatics of the U.S.S.R. held their Second National Trampoline Championships.

Twenty-five men, eighteen women and seventeen youths and fourteen girls born between the years 1949–1952 took part. The majority of the competitors took part in the higher category—for Masters of Sport. The eight men and eight women who competed in the final of the U.S.S.R. Championships performed the compulsory routine taken from the programme of the 1966 World Championships, as well as an optional routine. It is interesting to note the rapid improvement in the difficulty-rating of the routines performed at the competitions by the three prize-winners of the 1966 U.S.S.R. Championships.

Description of the optional trampoline routines performed at the 1966 U.S.S.R. Championships

MEN

1st. PALAGIN, VIKTOR—*Moscow*

> 1. Double back somersault.
> 2. Half-out fliffis.

3. Over turned Rudolph to Back Drop.
4. Back Pull-over
5. Back somersault.
6. Back one and three-quarter somersault.
7. Full twisting Cody.
8. Back somersault.
9. Back one and three-quarter somersault.
10. Double Back Cody.

2nd. STUKUSHIN, SERGEI—*Kiev*

1. Forward two and three-quarter somersault
   to Back Drop.
2. Ball-out Barani.
3. Rudolph.
4. Back one and three-quarter somersault.
5. Full twisting Cody.
6. Back somersault with full twist.
7. Double back somersault.
8. Half-out fliffis.
9. Rudolph.
10. Double back somersault.

3rd. LEVENCHUK, ALEKSANDR—*Minsk*

1. Double back somersault.
2. Forward one and three-quarter somersault
   with full-twist.
3. Rudy Ball-out.
4. Back somersault with full-twist.
5. Back somersault.
6. Back somersault with double-twist.
7. Rudolph.
8. Back somersault.
9. Back one and three-quarter somersault.
10. Double Back Cody.

LADIES

1st. ZDANYUK, LYUDMILA—*Minsk*

1. One and a quarter front somersault with
   full-twist to Front Drop.
2. Front Cody with half-twist.
3. Back somersault.
4. Back somersault with full-twist.
5. Barani.
6. One and a quarter back somersault to
   Back Drop.

7. Back Pull-over.
8. Back somersault with full-twist.
9. Lazy back.
10. Back Cody.

2nd. FEDOSOVA, TAMARA—*Moscow*

1. Barani.
2. Crash dive.
3. Half-twist to feet.
4. Back somersault.
5. Barani.
6. Back somersault.
7. Back somersault with full-twist.
8. Front somersault.
9. Lazy back.
10. Back Cody.

3rd. ANTONOVA, MARINA—*Leningrad*

1. Barani.
2. Back Drop.
3. Half-twist to feet.
4. Back somersault.
5. Front somersault.
6. Back somersault with full-twist.
7. One and a quarter back somersault to Back Drop.
8. Back Pull-over.
9. Back somersault.
10. Double back somersault.

In November 1966 the British Trampoline Federation was asked to assist the Nissen Corporation in making the arrangements for the Nissen Cup Competition to be held at the Crystal Palace National Recreation Centre on 19th November.

This international competition is open to competitors all over the world and is second only to the World Championships themselves. Countries which sent competitors to these championships were Denmark, England, West Germany, Holland, Switzerland, United States of America and Wales.

The first ten competitors in each contest performed in the finals with the following results:

LADIES

1.	L. Ball	38·20	England
2.	B. John	37·75	England
3.	S. Vine	36·85	England
4.	J. Cramphorn	34·70	England
5.	M. Badgery	34·65	England
6.	W. Coulton	34·40	England
7.	L. Bevis	34·15	England
8.	D. Bullen	33·50	England
9.	M. Ratcliffe	29·10	England
10.	L. Abrahamsen	26·15	Denmark

MEN

1.	D. Jacobs	45·55	U.S.A.
2.	D. Curtis	42·50	Wales
3.	M. Williams	42·05	Wales
4.	H. Riehle	42·05	W. Germany
5.	D. Schulz	40·50	W. Germany
6.	K. Treiter	39·20	W. Germany
7.	J. Newton	39·05	England
8.	D. Lease	39·00	England
9.	S. McEneny	38·65	England
10.	P. Wainwright	37·70	England

SECOND BRITISH TRAMPOLINE FEDERATION NATIONAL CHAMPIONSHIPS, 1967

GIRLS

Name	Preliminary	Final	Tariff	Total	Position
D. Bullen	21·70	8·75	5·00	35·45	1
J. Cramphorn	20·50	8·85	4·20	33·55	2
L. Bevis	20·20	8·45	4·10	32·75	3
J. Reed	19·40	8·15	4·70	32·25	4
J. Vaughan	18·15	8·05	3·70	29·90	5

BOYS

Name	Preliminary	Final	Tariff	Total	Position
R. Hughes	22·50	8·10	5·50	36·10	1
P. Luxon	22·15	8·10	5·30	35·55	2
T. Hall	21·45	7·30	5·30	34·45	3
P. Wade	21·20	7·30	5·30	33·80	4
M. Cable	20·75	6·90	5·80	33·45	5

LADIES

Name	Preliminary	Final	Tariff	Total	Position
B. John	23·65	8·80	6·00	38·45	1
S. Vine	23·40	8·25	6·30	37·95	2
D. Bullen	22·40	8·55	6·20	37·15	3
W. Coulton	22·15	8·45	5·80	36·40	4
M. Badgery	21·45	8·50	4·60	34·55	5

The most disappointing thing about the nationals this year was the fact that Lynda Ball, the reigning British champion and our most successful lady competitor, did not enter the championship because she was unable to perform one of the movements for the compulsory routine.

MEN

Name	Preliminary	Final	Tariff	Total	Position
D. Curtis	26·80	8·70	8·70	44·20	1
C. Brigden	20·05	8·30	8·30	41·65	2
M. Williams	25·50	8·80	7·30	41·60	3
R. Hughes	22·70	8·15	6·70	37·55	4
R. Holland	23·50	6·85	6·60	36·95	5

On Saturday, 17th June 1967, the Fourth World Championships were held at the Crystal Palace National Recreation Centre, London. Competitors from nine different countries took part in the championships comprising nine entries in the Ladies' section and sixteen in the Men's section.

In the Ladies' competition that invincible performer, Judy Wills, again took the title for the fourth successive year. Judy was in a class of her own. Her repertoire of movements and the degree of difficulty of her competitive routine make her a very difficult performer to beat. When her reign does finally end we may have witnessed a performer whose undefeated record may stand for all time. Britain's number one representative, Lynda Ball, had the misfortune to be injured in a car accident the week before the championship and, therefore, could not compete. Her place was taken by Wendy Coulton who represented Britain the year before in America.

The result of the finalists was as follows:

		Com- pulsory	1st Vol.	2nd Vol.	Total
1. Judy Wills	U.S.A.	9·25	17·55	17·90	44·70
2. Nancy Smith	U.S.A.	8·90	15·65	16·75	41·30
3. Charlene Paletz	South Africa	8·90	15·70	15·90	40·50
4. Ute Czech	West Germany	9·05	15·15	14·50	38·70
5. Sue Vine	Great Britain	8·90	14·65	15·05	38·60
6. Wendy Coulton	Great Britain	8·70	14·75	14·65	38·10
7. Agathe Jarosch	West Germany	9·20	13·05	15·20	37·45
8. Linda Dinkleman	South Africa	9·15	—	15·15	24·30
9. Ria Belt	Holland	—	14·60	2·60	17·20

The most improved performer in this section was Charlene Paletz who after the first voluntary routines was in second place. Last year she finished seventh.

Unfortunately in the Men's section the defending World Champion, Wayne Miller, had a foot injury and could not compete. Jimmy Yongue of Lafayette, Louisiana was his substitute. It is interesting to note that in the Women's competition Judy Wills has captured the title every year since its inception, whereas in the Men's competition not only has there been a new champion each year but also the previous champion has been unable to represent his country in order to defend his title.

The final positions were as follows:

		Com- pulsory	1st Vol.	2nd Vol.	Total
1. Dave Jacobs	U.S.A.	9·60	18·60	18·50	46·70
2. Dave Curtis	Great Britain	8·95	17·95	17·20	44·10
3. Mike Williams	Great Britain	9·15	17·60	16·95	43·70
4. Kurt Treiter	West Germany	9·00	16·75	17·20	42·95
5. Hartmut Riehle	West Germany	9·00	16·90	16·95	42·85
6. Ron Abbott	South Africa	9·00	15·90	16·85	41·75
7. Ian McNaughton	South Africa	9·25	16·10	15·75	41·10
8. Jimmy Yongue	U.S.A.	9·50	17·60	12·85	39·95
9. Hil Van Dierman	Holland	8·05	14·40	14·35	36·80
10. Kurt Höhener	Switzerland	9·05	16·60	—	25·65

The most improved performers in the Men's section were undoubtedly the British pair Dave Curtis and Mike Williams.

The results of the two competitions confirm that the four leading nations are U.S.A., Great Britain, West Germany and South Africa.

The Synchronized Team Competition created many upsets in

performance, but once again the American girls showed their mastery of the situation and the title remained in their possession.

The result of the Men's competition was delayed pending a protest over performance differences. The final results published were:

LADIES' SYNCHRONIZED

1. U.S.A.   15·25
2. West Germany 13·60
3. Great Britain   12·70
4. South Africa   12·55

MEN'S SYNCHRONIZED

1. West Germany 14·70
2. Switzerland   14·30
3. South Africa   13·25
4. U.S.A.   6·40
5. Holland   5·95
6. Great Britain   —

The Fifth World Championships will be held in Amersfoort, Holland, on 30th November and 1st December 1968. The same year an exhibition team will demonstrate the art of trampolining during the Olympic Games in Mexico City. At each Olympic Games the host nation is allowed to select two new sports to be included in the Games programme. In 1972 the Olympic Games will be held in Munich, and since Germany is one of the leading countries in this sport they have every intention that one of their selections for these Olympic Games will be trampolining.

12

Rules and Regulations

International Rules
for Trampoline Competitions

1. International trampoline competitions shall consist of one compulsory and one voluntary routine. The ten best participants shall be admitted to the final and in the final they have to perform their voluntary routine once more.
2. The starting order of the competitors will be decided by a draw. This starting order applies only for the compulsory exercises. The ranking position based on the results of the compulsory routines will decide the starting order for the voluntary routines. The competitor with the lowest marks starts first. There has to be a break between the compulsory and voluntary routines.
3. The compulsory and voluntary routines shall consist of ten movements as published in the official announcements.
4. The compulsory and voluntary routines cannot be repeated.
5. No skills may be repeated in voluntary routines. The penalty for a repeated stunt is that the difficulty rating for the repeated stunt is deducted from the difficulty of the whole routine.
6. The referee and assistant referee shall determine the difficulty values of the voluntary routines.
7. All jumps are named and difficulty graded in a tariff table (see no. 32).
8. All routines shall be performed unaided and only the official spotters shall be allowed to stand around the trampoline.
9. The jury consist of:

one referee
one assistant referee
four judges
one recorder.

10. The jury members for international competitions must be approved by the F.I.T.
11. The referee shall only vote when a disagreement is involved (see nos. 17, 24, 26).
12. The judges shall be placed at least five metres from the apparatus and to the side, on raised seat.
13. Trampoline routines shall be marked by tenths of points.
14. The number of points gained by a competitor shall be the total of the marks gained for 'performance' plus the 'tariff value'.
15. The judges shall mark the performance publicly and independently by using marking cards that must be simultaneously displayed immediately on the referee's signal.
16. The judges mark only the 'performance' of a routine up to 10 points.
17. When one judge fails to display his marks simultaneously with the other judges then an average mark of the other judges will be taken as the value for the exercise. The decision about this will be made by the referee.
18. The difficulty value for the voluntary routine is the total sum of the difficulty marks for each jump performed in the routine.
19. The jury should do some trial scoring in advance of the actual competition.
20. The referee counts each contact with the bed after first movement of the routine, as follows:
    1—2—3 . . . 9—10—out.
21. The recorder makes a note of the marks awarded, crosses out the highest and the lowest and takes the average of the remaining two marks. He then adds the degree of difficulty to the performance marks, makes deductions as indicated by the referee and records the final score for the routine.
22. The judges shall assess performance from the following points of view:

(a) form

(b) execution

(c) control.

23. Competitors with the same marks will be given the same placing in the results. If a winner is needed (say for a cup or annual challenge trophy), a jump-off shall be held using a voluntary routine.

24. If the difference between the two middle performance marks given by the judges is more than 0·5 points, a special discussion by the jury shall follow.

25. Judges will make the following deductions for faulty performance:

(a) For each part of the routine:

insufficient height	0·1—0·5 points
lack of form	0·1—0·5 points
poor execution (arrangement, rhythm)	0·1—0·5 points

(b) For the routine as a whole:

lack of control after last bounce (safety)	0·1—1·0 points

26. If the competitor touches with any part of his body the frame or the suspension system, he shall be scored only on the basis of the number of skills (routine parts) he has completed up to that time.

27. If the competitor falls off the trampoline or must be held on by the spotters his score shall be zero points.

28. If the competitor changes the compulsory routines he will be penalized by losing 1·0 points for each wrong or missing exercise. The points deductions will be made by the referee.

29. If a competitor shows a noticeable change in rhythm or stops his exercise the judges will mark him for the executed movements only (i.e. six movements completed = maximum 6 points). The referee will decide the difficulty mark up to that time.

30. The exercise terminates with a feet landing after the tenth movement but the competitor is allowed one more jump in a stretched position. If the competitor does not land on his

feet after the tenth bounce, judges have to make a deduction for lack of control from 0·1—1·0 points.

The following deductions are as a guide:

(a) An additional step forward or backward after landing 0·1—0·3 points.

(b) Touching the bed with the hand after landing but still standing 0·4—0·5 points.

(c) Landing or falling on knees or seat 0·6—0·7 points.

(d) Landing or falling on back or stomach 0·7—1·0 points.

31. Competition Rules for Synchronized Trampoling.

The referee and assistant referee check the simultaneous jumps and record the difficulty.

Judges 1 and 2 are judging the form on trampoline No. 1.

Judges 3 and 4 are judging form on trampoline No. 2. The average mark is calculated as in individual competitions.

Synchronized judges Nos. 5 and 6 judge independently of each other the executing of the sychronized exercise. They make deductions for the different landings from 0·1—0·5 points.

The average of both marks will be the deduction for the faulty synchronized exercise, i.e.:

Average of four form judges	8·9 points
Difficulty (Referee)	6·0 points
	——
	14·9 points
Average of two synchronized judges	1·5 points
	——
	13·4 points
	——

32. *Performance Regulations:*

(a) He shall start on the signal given by the referee.

(b) The competitor takes as many preliminary jumps as he desires before commencing the first movement of his routine.

(c) The legs shall be closed after leaving the bed and shall remain in this stretched position while the performer is in the air.

(d) The legs have to be properly stretched, tucked or piked, as the case may be for each movement.

(e) In the tucked position, the body should be rolled up closely with the knees tight together. The hands grasp the legs below the knees.

(f) For combination movements (somersaults with twists) the competitor himself may decide in which phase he will perform the twist, if the table in degree of difficulty does not warrant otherwise.

(g) Fliffes may, although being the same skill, be performed in different ways. These skills are classed as different tricks but still have the same difficulty rating.

33. *Explanation of the table on degree of difficulty.*

(a) The difficulty grades in this table (1—15) are in tenths of points.

(b) The degree of difficulty for every jump is worked out on the following principle.

Quarter of a somersault (90°)	= 0·10 point
Somersault (360°)	= 0·40 point
Half-twist (180°)	= 0·10 point
Full-twist (360°)	= 0·20 point

(c) Piked and layout skills of 360° of rotation are marked on an extra 0·10 difficulty for the position if they are not executed with a twist.

(d) Tucked, piked and layout jumps are considered as different jumps and not as repetitions.

(e) The same goes for the twists and multiple somersaults.

(f) Double somersaults with a half-twist in the first, middle or last phase have the same degree of difficulty, but are considered as being different jumps.

34. All written protests given to the referee must be accompanied by a $10 deposit. If these protests are accepted, then the deposit is returned; if not, the amount goes into the accounts of the organizing body. Protests can be made only by the team manager and will be discussed immediately the competition is over. The decision of the jury will be publicly displayed.

RULES AND REGULATIONS

Technical Regulations

Spotters

For each competition the organizer must provide four spotters who are experienced in their job.

Marks

In each competition the marks will be announced after each exercise before the next competitor goes on the trampoline.

Clothing

The men have to wear a sports vest, trousers and trampoline shoes. The women must wear leotard and trampoline slippers.

Judges

For each judge there must be a recorder for writing down deductions.

Repetition of Exercises

The referee can, together with the judges through a majority vote, ask a competitor to repeat the routine, but only if the competitor is obviously disturbed by flashlights, undue noise, etc.

Competition Card

All competitors must write and hand in their intended exercise in good time. Alteration to this exercise is allowed.

Voluntary

If a competitor finishes his exercise before the tenth move the referee has to deduct one point from the final marks for each missing skill.

World Championships

(a) At the World Championships there is to be a videotape recorder. Through the reshowing there will be an exact control of the exercises performed over which there would normally be a possible disagreement.

(b) Technical committee suggest that the World Championship medal will be presented with a coloured ribbon.

(c) *Synchronized Trampolining.* The competitors for the synchronized competition do not have to take part in the individual competition. Each nation can have four men and four women for the World Championships.

(d) *Warm Up.* The warm-up session in the competition hall shall commence one hour before the start of the championships. However, there should be an additional hall for the performers to warm up before the competition begins.

THE AXIAL ROTATION SYSTEM

The difficulty ratings of the international rules are based upon the axial rotation system. This system has been developed through a great deal of work on the part of Bob Bollinger of Rockford, Illinois, U.S.A., whose study on axial rotation won for him the C. H. McCloy Research Award at the 1964 National Gymnastic Clinic in Sarasota, Florida. Since the international committee made certain amendments to the original system I have outlined the original here for comparison.

The difficulty rating is based upon the degree of rotation about the axes of the body. Since the lowest number of degrees passed through on any given competition movement is 90°, one mark is awarded for each quarter of a somersault completed. Therefore, for movements such as Front Drop and Back Drop, one mark is given. For single somersaults, four marks are awarded and so on. When it comes to twists about the longitudinal axis, the minimum amount of twist performed normally is one half only. Therefore, one mark is awarded for each half-twist completed. Combinations of twists and somersaults are still scored on the same method: a Barani would score five points (four for the somersault and one for the half-twist). A double twisting backward somersault would score eight (four for the somersault and four for the double-twist). A bonus point is awarded where the take-off is from the Front or Back Drop position rather than from the feet and where somersaults are performed in a straight or piked position. Because a movement can be made increasingly more difficult when performed in swingtime, some allowance must be made for its combination value. A full twisting backward somersault is made more difficult when preceded by a double somersault than when performed from a single somersault. The combination difficulty value is calculated by using the following formula.

$$\text{Stunt B} = \text{Stunt B} + \frac{(\text{Stunt A} \times \text{Stunt B})}{10}$$

For example; imagine Stunt B to be the full twisting backward somersault and Stunt A the double backward somersault. The individual difficulty rating of Stunt B is equal to six (four for the somersault and two for the full-twist). The individual value of Stunt A is equal to eight (four points for each somersault). Therefore, when calculated in full, the combination difficulty rating is equal to 10·80.

$$\begin{aligned}
\text{Stunt B} &= 6 + \frac{(8 \times 6)}{10} \\
&= 6 + \frac{48}{10} \\
&= 6 + 4\cdot8 \\
&= 10\cdot8
\end{aligned}$$

Now let us take a complete routine and see how this works.

Movement	Individual difficulty rating	Combination difficulty rating	Total
1. Layout back somie	5	0	5·0
2. Barani	5	2·5	7·5
3. Full twisting back	6	3·0	9·0
4. Rudolph	7	4·2	11·2
5. Back somie (c)	4	2·8	6·8
6. Double back (c)	8	3·2	11·2
7. Barani	5	4·0	9·0
8. Double twisting back	8	4·0	12·0
9. Back somie (b)	5	4·0	9·0
10. ½-in ½-out fliffis	10	5·0	15·0
Total	63	32·7	95·7

The use of this system is invaluable for the following:
(a) seeding performers in a Knock-Out tournament;
(b) as an objective training aid in progressional learning;
(c) the compiling of competition routines;
(d) a method of listing and ranking performers in clubs, regions, nationally or internationally;
(e) a means whereby judges can decide winners in a Knock-Out competition.

THE KNOCK-OUT SYSTEM

Another method of running a competition is by using the Knock-Out system. The most satisfactory type is the double elimination tournament whereby each competitor must be defeated twice before being eliminated. The competitors are seeded invariably by using the axial rotation system, so that the competition is both thrilling and satisfying.

When a competitor loses against his opponent, he automatically enters the consolation bracket where he still has the opportunity of competing against the winner of the original bracket. Should the winner of the ordinary bracket meet with his first defeat in the grand final, a rematch will be held between the two to determine the outright winner.

RULES AND REGULATIONS

An example of the double elimination Knock-Out procedure is set out here for your guidance.

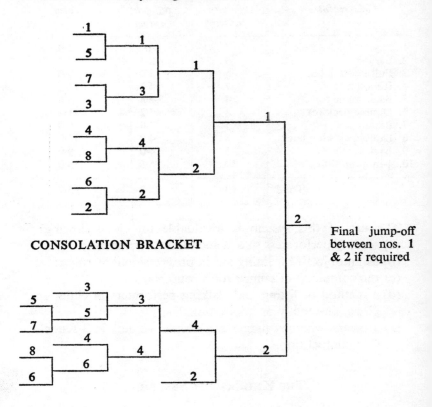

CONSOLATION BRACKET

Final jump-off between nos. 1 & 2 if required

Starting Positions

Somersault	Twist	Feet Forward	Feet Backward	Feet Pike	Feet Layout	Seat Forward	Seat Backward	Seat Pike	Seat Layout	Stomach Forward	Stomach Backward	Stomach Pike	Stomach Layout	Back Forward	Back Backward	Back Pike	Back Layout
Tuck Jump		1	—	—	—	—	—	—	—	—	—	—	—	—	—	—	—
Pike Jump		1	—	—	—	—	—	—	—	—	—	—	—	—	—	—	—
Pike Jump		1	—	—	—	—	—	—	—	—	—	—	—	—	—	—	—
Pike Straddle Jump		1	—	—	—	—	—	—	—	—	—	—	—	—	—	—	—
Split Jump		1	—	—	—	—	—	—	—	—	—	—	—	—	—	—	—
All similar jumps without twists		1	—	—	—	—	—	—	—	—	—	—	—	—	—	—	—
Seat bounce		1	—	—	—	1	—	—	—	—	—	—	—	—	—	—	—
Turntables ½		—	—	—	—	—	—	—	—	—	1	—	—	—	—	—	—
Turntables 1		—	—	—	—	—	—	—	—	—	2	—	—	—	—	—	—
Turntables 1½		—	—	—	—	—	—	—	—	—	3	—	—	—	—	—	—
Turntables 2		—	—	—	—	—	—	—	—	—	4	—	—	—	—	—	—
0	½	—	—	—	—	—	—	—	—	—	—	1	—	—	—	1	—
0	1	—	—	—	—	2	—	—	—	—	—	2	—	—	—	2	—
0	1½	—	—	—	—	—	—	—	—	—	—	3	—	—	—	3	—
0	2	—	—	—	—	4	—	—	—	—	—	4	—	—	—	4	—
0	2½	—	—	—	—	—	—	—	—	—	—	5	—	—	—	5	—
0	3	—	—	—	—	6	—	—	—	—	—	6	—	—	—	6	—
½	0	1	1	—	—	—	—	—	—	—	1	—	—	1	—	—	—
½	½	2	2	—	—	2	—	—	—	—	2	—	—	2	—	—	—
½	1	3	3	—	—	—	—	—	—	—	3	—	—	3	—	—	—
½	1½	4	4	—	—	4	—	—	—	—	4	—	—	4	—	—	—
½	2	5	5	—	—	—	—	—	—	—	5	—	—	5	—	—	—
½	2½	6	6	—	—	6	—	—	—	—	6	—	—	6	—	—	—
½	3	7	7	—	—	—	—	—	—	—	7	—	—	7	—	—	—

Somersault	Twist	Feet Forward	Feet Backward	Feet Pike	Feet Layout	Seat Forward	Seat Backward	Seat Pike	Seat Layout	Stomach Forward	Stomach Backward	Stomach Pike	Stomach Layout	Back Forward	Back Backward	Back Pike	Back Layout
½	0	—	—	—	—	—	—	—	—	2	2	—	—	2	2	—	—
½	½	—	—	—	—	—	—	—	—	3	3	—	—	3	3	—	—
½	1	—	—	—	—	—	—	—	—	4	4	—	—	4	4	—	—
½	1½	—	—	—	—	—	—	—	—	5	5	—	—	5	5	—	—
½	2	—	—	—	—	—	—	—	—	6	6	—	—	6	6	—	—
½	2½	—	—	—	—	—	—	—	—	7	7	—	—	7	7	—	—
½	3	—	—	—	—	—	—	—	—	8	8	—	—	8	8	—	—
1	0	3	3	3	3	3	3	—	—	3	—	—	—	—	3	—	—
1	½	4	4	Free	—	4	4	—	—	4	—	—	—	—	4	—	—
1	1	5	5	Free	—	5	5	—	—	5	—	—	—	—	5	—	—
1	1½	6	6	Free	—	6	6	—	—	6	—	—	—	—	6	—	—
1	2	7	7	Free	—	7	7	—	—	7	—	—	—	—	7	—	—
1	2½	8	8	Free	—	8	8	—	—	8	—	—	—	—	8	—	—
1	3	9	9	Free	—	9	9	—	—	9	—	—	—	—	9	—	—
1	0	4	4	5	5	4	4	—	—	4	4	5	5	4	4	—	—
1	½	5	5	Free	—	5	5	—	—	5	5	—	—	5	5	—	—
1	1	6	6	Free	—	6	6	—	—	6	6	—	—	6	6	—	—
1	1½	7	7	Free	—	7	7	—	—	7	7	—	—	7	7	—	—
1	2	8	8	Free	—	8	8	—	—	8	8	—	—	8	8	—	—
1	2½	9	9	Free	—	9	9	—	—	9	9	—	—	9	9	—	—
1	3	10	10	Free	—	10	10	—	—	10	10	—	—	—	—	—	—
1	3½	11	11	Free	—	—	—	—	—	—	—	—	—	—	—	—	—

				Fwd P.L.	Back P.L.												
1—¼	1	7	7	Free		—	—	—	—	—	7	—	—	7	—	—	—
1—¼	1—½	8	8	Free		8	—	—	—	—	8	—	—	8	—	—	—
1—¼	2	9	9	Free		—	—	—	—	—	9	—	—	9	—	—	—
1—¼	2—½	10	10	Free		10	—	—	—	—	10	—	—	10	—	—	—
1—¼	3	11	11	Free		—	—	—	—	—	11	—	—	11	—	—	—
1—¼	3—½	12	12	Free		—	—	—	—	—	12	—	—	12	—	—	—
1—¼	4	13	13	Free		—	—	—	—	—	13	—	—	—	—	—	—
1—½	0	—	—	—	—		—	—	6	6	7	7	6	6	—	—
1—½	½	—	—	—	—		—	—	7	7	—	—	7	7	—	—
1—½	1	—	—	—	—		—	—	8	8	—	—	8	8	—	—
1—½	1—½	—	—	—	—		—	—	9	9	—	—	9	9	—	—
1—½	2	—	—	—	—		—	—	10	10	—	—	10	10	—	—
1—½	2—½	—	—	—	—		—	—	11	11	—	—	11	11	—	—
1—½	3	—	—	—	—		—	—	12	12	—	—	12	12	—	—
1—½	3—½	—	—	—	—		—	—	13	13	—	—	—	—	—	—
1—½	4	—	—	—	—		—	—	—	—	—	—	—	—	—	—

				Fwd P.L.	Back P.L.												
				8 8	8 8												
1—¾	0	7	7	Free	Free	7	7	—	—	7	—	8	8	—	7	—	—
1—¾	½	8	8	Free	Free	8	8	—	—	8	—	—	—	—	8	—	—
1—¾	1	9	11	Free	Free	9	9	—	—	9	—	—	—	—	9	—	—
1—¾	1—½	10	10	Free	Free	10	10	—	—	10	—	—	—	—	10	—	—
1—¾	2	11	13	Free	Free	—	—	—	—	—	—	—	—	—	11	—	—
1—¾	2—½	12	12	Free	Free	—	—	—	—	—	—	—	—	—	—	—	—
1—¾	3	13	15	Free	Free	—	—	—	—	—	—	—	—	—	—	—	—
1—¾	3—½	14	14	Free	Free	—	—	—	—	—	—	—	—	—	—	—	—

2	0	8	8	9	9	8	8	—	—	8	8	9	9	8	8	—	—
2	½	9	9	Free		9	9	—	—	9	9	—	—	9	9	—	—
2	1	10	10	Free		—	—	—	—	10	10	—	—	10	10	—	—
2	1—½	11	11	Free	—	—	—	—	—	—	11	—	—	11	—	—	—
2	2	12	12	Free		—	—	—	—	—	12	—	—	12	—	—	—
2	2—½	13	13	Free		—	—	—	—	—	—	—	—	—	—	—	—
2	3	14	14	Free		—	—	—	—	—	—	—	—	—	—	—	—
2	3—½	15	15	Free		—	—	—	—	—	—	—	—	—	—	—	—

		Feet				Seat				Stomach				Back			
Somersault	Twist	Forward	Backward	Pike	Layout	Forward	Backward	Pike	Layout	Forward	Backward	Pike	Layout	Forward	Backward	Pike	Layout
2¼	0	9	9	10	10	—	—	—	—	—	9	10	10	9	—	—	—
2¼	½	10	10	Free	—	—	—	—	—	—	10	—	—	10	—	—	—
2¼	1	11	11	Free	—	—	—	—	—	—	11	—	—	11	—	—	—
2¼	1½	—	—	—	—	—	—	—	—	—	12	—	—	12	—	—	—
2¼	2	—	—	—	—	—	—	—	—	—	13	—	—	—	—	—	—
2½	0	—	—	—	—	—	—	—	—	10	10	11	11	10	10	—	—
2½	½	—	—	—	—	—	—	—	—	11	11	—	—	11	11	—	—
2½	1	—	—	—	—	—	—	—	—	12	12	—	—	12	12	—	—
2¾	0	11	11	12	12	—	—	—	—	—	—	—	—	—	—	—	—
2¾	½	12	12	Free	Free	—	—	—	—	—	—	—	—	—	—	—	—
2¾	1	13	15	Free	Free	—	—	—	—	—	—	—	—	—	—	—	—
3	0	12	12	13	13	—	—	—	—	—	12	—	—	12	—	—	—
3	½	13	—	Free	—	—	—	—	—	—	—	—	—	—	—	—	—
3	1	14	14	Free	—	—	—	—	—	—	—	—	—	—	—	—	—
3	1½	15	—	—	—	—	—	—	—	—	—	—	—	—	—	—	—
3¼	0	13	13	14	14	—	—	—	—	—	13	—	—	13	—	—	—

(Feet, Pike/Layout, 2¾ somersault group annotated: Fwd Back / P. L. P. L. / 12 12 / Free Free / Free Free)

13

Organizing a Competition

I am endeavouring here to set out certain notes which it is hoped may serve as a useful guide to committees and officials who have undertaken the task of organizing their first competition. It is not suggested that the advice offered here should be strictly adhered to since local circumstances may require that some points be modified.

Organizing Committee. Should a club or association wish to make all the arrangements for the proposed competition, then a sub-committee can be formed and various responsibilities delegated to the members of this sub-committee. Any organization not specifically connected with the British Trampoline Federation but proposing to organize its own competition would do well to contact the assistant secretary of the British Trampoline Federation to ask if any local officials might be able to assist either practically or in an advisory capacity.

Organizing Secretary. Whenever possible this should be a person with previous experience as an administrator or, failing this, someone who has spent a great deal of his time mixing with competitors, coaches and officials and, therefore, understands something of each of their feelings and contributions to the sport. This person will have a great deal of work to accomplish and so must be able to devote an enormous amount of time to this alone. He must be capable, enthusiastic, patient and far-sighted.

Honorary Treasurer. With any project where money is involved there must be a person to take full responsibility for keeping a discriminating eye on income and expenditure. This

217

person must obviously have some accounting knowledge. The treasurer, possibly together with the secretary, should open an account at a bank in the name of the club or association. With advice from the bank manager it can be decided whose signatures will be acceptable on cheques when money has to be withdrawn. One signature will always be that of the treasurer together with one other from two or three approved by the organizing committee.

Since the secretary will have to act on certain procedures at a moment's notice, a float of ready available cash must be made to him. Receipts must be obtained for any purchase of any amount and a detailed record of all expenses including postage and telephone calls must be kept. It is a good idea for the treasurer to make a habit of paying into the bank all receipts as soon as possible, as it is not impossible for cheques and postal orders to be mislaid and lost among all the other pieces of paper that accumulate when an important competition is being arranged. Remember also that postal orders become invalid if not cashed within six calendar months from the date of issue. If admission to the competition is not by ticket only and an admission fee has to be paid at the door, then trustworthy officials should be appointed and supplied with adequate small change. This also applies to programme sellers.

Preparation. The first, and possibly one of the most important, factors is the chosen venue for the competition. The building must have adequate height to the ceiling, at least 25 ft., so that performers may bounce in safety. There must be adequate changing facilities, showers and toilets. Toilets must also be made available to the spectators. An estimate must be made as to the number of spectators likely to attend and sufficient seating accommodation must be available. If the attendance of a large audience is one of the desires of the organizing committee, then a venue which is easily accessible by all modes of transport must be selected carefully. Before making any definite booking of a hall, make inquiries as to whether there might be any counter-attraction on the same date of your proposed choice. The local Press is usually able to help in this direction. By selecting the wrong date, what could have been a most successful meeting

218

may turn out to be a flop. For big meetings, the police, Automobile Association and the Royal Automobile Club should be informed. It may then be possible to call upon the police to control the traffic entering the town and at main entrances and exits to the parking areas. The A.A. and R.A.C. may wish to display special signs to direct the traffic along the correct route.

The number and type of individual competitions must be resolved and a decision made as to whether compulsory routines are required and, if so, how these should be composed. All existing trophies should be recalled from the holders before the date of the competition just in case they are forgotten on the big day or in case slight repairs need to be carried out. Where new trophies are required it might be possible to obtain these by writing to, or visiting personally, the managers of sports companies or industrial and commercial concerns and asking if they would care to donate the prizes. Local M.P.s or councillors are others who may be able to assist in this way.

A programme must be prepared setting out details of the competitions. It is most useful if the names of the competitors are listed in the order of performance and the names of the holders of the titles printed in some appropriate position. The scoring system to be used should also be included in the programme together with a scoring chart for the results. The names of the officials, a list of the trophies with the names of the donors and the name of the person making the presentations to the winners must be displayed prominently.

Printing. The preparation of the programme requires a great deal of thought. If the secretary has never planned one before, he should obtain copies of programmes from other meetings and use these as a guide. An outline of the programme giving as much detail as possible should be prepared and the number of pages assessed. Estimates should be obtained from printers, carefully selecting the quality of paper required. When the committee has decided which estimate to accept, the secretary should consult the printer and agree upon the date when the copy should be presented to be set up; the proofs will be available; proofs should be returned; and when delivery of the printed programme is to be made. The printer can set up the programme in advance, except the names of the competitors and their order of jumping. Proof checking should not be left to the printer since he may not have the specialized knowledge required and, therefore, the secretary should check the proofs. Advertisers will wish to see proofs and they must be given a date for returning them. Alterations at proof stage increase cost; the copy, therefore, must be clear and carefully and finally drafted before being sent to the printer. If entrance to the competition is by programme only, it is necessary to have delivery of these in plenty of time to distribute and sell. Copies should be sent to all officials, competitors, the announcer, the persons from whom the building has been hired, donors of trophies, dignitaries who will be present and the Press. Permission to display posters must be sought from shopkeepers, libraries and the local council.

All the officials should be given refreshments either on arrival, which will give them an opportunity to discuss any points on running the competitions, or when the show is over and lessons are noted which will assist greatly in making the next presentation even more of a success than the one just terminated. Refreshments should also be made available to the general public during an interval or after the competitions.

The organizing secretary must contact, as soon as possible, the officials he wishes to assist him in the running of the production so that they can set aside the proposed date in their diaries. The minimum number of officials would be the following. One *Referee* who should be the most experienced person available. He must be able to guide the judges towards displaying marks suitable for the performance witnessed, and make certain that there is never a great discrepancy between these. It is for this reason that the referee normally calls upon a performer to set the standard before the actual competition. It is quite useless calling upon *any* competitor to perform this service since it gives no indication of what might be expected from the other performers. When it is necessary to set a standard, the best known bouncer should be asked to perform. If the entire list of competitors is unknown to the officials then the entrants can be asked to disclose the content of their voluntary routines. This can be done easily in a general manner by asking questions such

as, 'Which of you is performing a fliffis in his voluntary routine?'
If more than one can identify himself in this category then
further questions can be asked such as, 'How many different
types of fliffis?', 'How many double somersaults?', 'How many
twisters?' Where the international rules are used, the referee
counts aloud each contact the performer makes with the bed and
together with his assistant is responsible for recording each
movement as it is performed and calculating the degree of difficulty for each routine. The referee must be so experienced that
in matters of discrepancy he can make a decision fairly and
confidently without having second thoughts. The whole meeting, once it has commenced, is entirely under his jurisdiction
and any decisions he makes are final.

Normally four *Judges* are required to assist the referee in
bringing the competitions to a favourable conclusion. These
adjudicators, if not qualified judges of trampolining, must have
experience in deciding on the relative merits of physical activities. Therefore, professional physical educationists should be
asked to perform this duty rather than notable inhabitants who
have been invited because of their names and status.

The job of the *Counter* if one is used is to assist the referee in
recording the number of contacts a performer makes with the
bed. Any deviation from the required number will result in a
loss of marks. Since the referee has to concentrate on checking
that the movements set out in the compulsory routine are performed in the correct order, he may need an assistant to count
these contacts audibly. By doing this the counter corroborates
the referee's calculations and also aids the performer should he
'lose' himself. The referee may wish to confer with the counter
on occasions and since his sole job is noting the number of contacts made with the bed, irrespective of which stunt was performed, the referee usually accepts whatever number the counter
states. Whatever the result, the decision of the referee is final.

Two *Calculators*, or scorers, are required to write down the
marks displayed by the judges for each performance. Usually
the highest and the lowest marks are deleted and the mean of
the remainder is recorded as the performer's score. This number
is added to the previous mark of the bouncer and an accumula-

221

tive score is also registered. Throughout the competitions time should be allowed for these successive scores to be announced after each performer. The reason for two calculators is so that one can always test the accuracy of the other.

Irrespective of the standard of the contest, four *Spotters* should always be in attendance around the trampoline. Their duties have been outlined in the chapter on Safety Precautions and, therefore, I will not repeat myself here.

Having decided upon the officials for the competition, experience proves that it is necessary to invite a duplicate set of officials in order to cover any unforeseen circumstances and also to give each member a rest. It would be most helpful if a short list of the duties of each official could be sent to him when confirmation of his acceptance to assist with the project has been received. Included with these duties should be a programme, the rules and regulations under which the competition is being run, the complete lists of compulsory routines to be performed by each competitor, directions on how to get to the venue, and a timetable for the officials. This timetable should give details of the preparatory meeting of the officials, proposed starting times of each individual competition, tea breaks, demonstrations, the awarding of the trophies and the terminating meeting of the officials to sum-up the proceedings and glean useful information for the next competition.

Stewards. The number you require will depend upon the size of the undertaking and the ingredients of its organization. If tickets have been issued or are to be sold, then there must be stewards at each entrance to carry out the appropriate duty. If the auditorium has been divided into sections and different fees are required for each section, or seats can be bookable, then another group of stewards must be on hand to direct people to their seats. It is usually much better to make the spectators' entry into the hall by programme only and the fee added on to the price of the programme. In this way there is a saving of the tax which is payable on all tickets but not on programmes, and fewer stewards are required to carry out the duties that are involved when tickets are issued and programmes have to be sold. There must be a **Chief Steward** who should be responsible for

222

keeping a record of the number of programmes issued to stewards, and ensuring that the money handed in tallies with the number of unsold programmes. Sometimes it is possible to secure the services of recognized voluntary organizations for some of these duties.

Press Steward. One person should be responsible for the Press representatives and a section of the hall should be reserved for them. A good relationship should always be maintained with the Press because they can do a great deal of good work in giving the sport publicity which in turn can lead to greater support from the general public. The Press steward should always be on hand to answer all inquiries from the reporters. The steward should, therefore, obtain as much information about the competitors as possible in order to carry out his duties properly.

Officials' Steward. This person should meet the officials on arrival and issue them with their badges of office. If refreshments are available at this time, then the steward should accompany the officials to the room allocated for this purpose and introduce them to any new faces. After the initial reception, the steward should then remain near to hand so that he can deal with any request from the officials.

Trophy Steward. Naturally, all the trophies will be on display and the steward's job is to act as a custodian against any damage or loss. During the awards at the end of the competition he must make sure that he hands the correct trophy to the person making the presentation.

Competitors' Stewards. At least two stewards are required for both the men and the women to assist in making sure the competitors know their order of bouncing and are ready beside the trampoline in good time. These stewards are also responsible for ensuring that each performer has his or her correct number attached securely to the chest and back. A report on any competitors who have scratched from their event should be sent to the referee, the announcer, the calculators and the Press as soon as the information is known.

Apparatus Stewards. The actual number you require will depend upon the size of the competition and the amount of apparatus to be used. The work of these people is to see that all equipment is in the correct place at the right time. The types of items for which they will be responsible will be trampolines, frame-pads, tables, chairs, score sheets, judging cards, pencils, whistle, bell, public replay equipment, videotape recorder, notices, blackboards, chalk, duster, and any music played on records or tape for providing a pleasant atmosphere for the audience before and after the competition and during any breaks. They will also be responsible for fanfare music for the presentations to the winners, and for smoothing-over all the little and not-so-little incidents which seem to occur at the wrong moment.

Area Controller. Here we have one of the most important people in making sure that the whole programme runs through without any noticeable snags. He is the person usually behind the scenes carrying most of the problems but always coming up with the solutions. Without doubt he must be a man with great experience. His finger must be on the pulse of every aspect of the organization so that he is able to control and combine all the components. I always feel very sorry for this person because he does so much work to make the competitions a success but he never gets the opportunity to watch the excitement.

Announcer. It is desirable that all announcing be carried out with the use of a microphone. Public address equipment may be hired if not already installed at the venue of the competition. So much depends on the quick and accurate transmission of results to the public that the announcer must be selected with care. He should be experienced in using a microphone, not easily flustered, and have some technical knowledge of trampolining. An ex-performer, especially if he knows the leading competitors, is an admirable choice. He will require two or three assistants to keep him informed of results, names of non-starters, etc., and one assistant to keep detailed records of information supplied. If possible, loud speakers should be placed in the dressing-rooms and warm-up gymnasia.

Music. Experience has shown that it is very beneficial to have music available to be played through the loud speaker system under direct control of the announcer. Soft music playing in the background before the competition begins can usually set a relaxed atmosphere to the proceedings. A record of a military fanfare of trumpets can support the importance of the presentation of the trophies.

First Aid. Medical attention must always be available. Where possible an interested doctor should be invited to all competitions. The local branch of the St. John Ambulance Brigade or British Red Cross Society should also be asked to attend. Since these are voluntary bodies a donation can be forwarded to them when the treasurer is making out his final statements. Inquiries should be made as to what ambulance facilities are available in the district, and from the local hospital what facilities are available if required. This information should be sent to the medical officer before the meeting.

14

Trampoline Terminology

In every sport there are certain names and terms peculiar to each sport and trampolining is no different from the rest of them. The many terms used in this new sport have an American flavour because the sport originated in the U.S.A. and the lead in all new developments usually comes from there. Many of the terms used are to save the competitor from writing reams in order to explain the movements in his voluntary routine.

A.A.U. Amateur Athletic Union.

Acceleration The increase in the rate of velocity.

Adolph Forward somersault with three and a half twists.

Aeroplane Half-twist to Front Drop.

Angular momentum The motion of a body produced by multiplying the angular velocity by the moment of inertia.

Angular velocity Speed of rotation about a central point.

Axial Rotation System This is a system of determining the difficulty rating for movements by allowing one point for each forward or backward rotation of 90° and one point for every half-twist executed.

Baby Fliffis Any fliffis movement with a rebound somewhere along the way. The most common movement associated with this term is the Back Drop, early half-twist into a back somersault.

Back A slang term for a backward somersault.

Back Drop A basic landing on the trampoline made with the back only from the lumbar region to the shoulders.

Back-full Backward somersault with full-twist.

Back Pull-over From a Back Drop the legs are pulled (or pushed) over the head into a three-quarter somersault to feet.

B.A.G.A. British Amateur Gymnastic Association.

Ball-out One and a quarter forward somersault originating from a Back Drop.

Barani A forward somersault with half-twist, sighting the bed throughout. Other accepted spellings: Barany, Borany, Borani, Brandy, Brany.

Barani-in A multiple forward somersaulting movement with a half-twist in the first somersault.

Barani-out A multiple forward somersaulting movement with a half-twist in the last somersault.

Barrel roll A side somersault.

Bed The jumping and landing area which is suspended from the frame of the trampoline.

Blind When a performer cannot see his way through a movement.

Bluch Front Drop, half-twist to Front Drop. (Not a half turntable.)

Break To stop the recoil from the bed by flexing at the hips, knees and ankles.

B.T.F. British Trampoline Federation.

Build-up The free bounces leading up to the start of a routine.

Cast Sideways movement across the trampoline bed.

Cat-twist Back Drop, full-twist to Back Drop.

Centre of gravity The point about which all the parts of the body exactly balance each other.

Checking Absorbing the recoil from the bed by flexing at the hips, knees and ankles.

Cody Forward or backward rotation from a Front Drop take off. Also known as a Cote.

Control To be able to perform exactly what is required without loss of balance.

Corkscrew Back Drop, one and a half twists to Back Drop.

Corpse Flat Back Drop.

Cradle Back Drop, half-twist to Back Drop.

Crash dive A three-quarter forward somersault where the body is fully extended during its descent towards the bed.

Difficulty The product of a movement after calculating its rating based on the Axial Rotation method of evaluation.

Dismount The method used in getting from the trampoline bed to the floor.

Dorso-Ventral axis An imaginary line passing through the body from front to rear about which the body rotates when performing side somersaults and turntables.

Double A double somersault.

Double-full Backward somersault with double twist.

Doubles Two people bouncing on one trampoline at the same time.

Double-twister Back somersault with double-twist.

D.T.B. Deutschen Turner-Bund.

Early twist fliffis Any fliffis movement where the twist is performed in the first somersault.

Eccentric thrust A force applied to one side and away from the centre of the mass.

Fliffis Any double somersault, forward or backward with a twist. Also known as fliffus and fliff. The plural spelling is fliffes.

Flip Slang term for a somersault.

Force Any push or pull that changes the body's existing state.

Form The style and control of a performer during his execution of a movement or routine.

Free bounce A straight bounce where no movement is carried out whilst in the air.

Front A forward somersault.

Front Drop A basic landing made on the stomach whilst the body is in the fully extended position.

Full Describes the number of twists executed in a somersault, e.g. Front-full, Back-full.

Gain Movement along the bed in the opposite direction to which the stunt is being performed.

Gravity The force causing bodies to tend towards the centre of the earth.

Half Refers to the amount of twist executed in a somersault, e.g. Half-out fliffis.

Inertia The property of a body by which it persists in an existing state of rest or uniform motion in a straight line until some external force changes that state.

I.T.A. International Trampolining Association.

Jona back Early half-twist into a back somersault.

Kaboom A somersaulting action created through one part of the body landing just after another part of the body, thereby setting up rotation. E.g. A flat back landing with the heels making contact with the bed just after the back. The result is a backward rotation.

Kill The action of absorbing the recoil from the bed by flexing at the hips, knees and ankles.

Kip When a person depresses the bed just before the performer so that the suspension system is stretched beyond the normal amount. The performer will then receive added impetus allowing more height in which to execute the intended stunt.

Knee Drop A basic landing position on the knees and shafts of the lower leg with the rest of the body, from the knees upwards, in a vertical position.

Knock-Out System A simple method of elimination through man-to-man competition where one performer must defeat his opponent in order to advance to the next round.

Lateral axis An imaginary line drawn through the hips from left to right about which the body rotates during forward and backward somersaults.

Layout A position where the body is completely extended.

Log-roll Front Drop, full-twist to Front Drop.

Longitudinal axis An imaginary line drawn through the body from head to toe about which the body rotates during twisting movements.

Lost When the performer is unable to orientate himself whilst in the air.

Miller Triple-twisting double-back. (Named after the originator, Wayne Miller.)

Momentum The quantity of motion in a body, the product of the mass by the velocity.

Mount There are two meanings for this word: (a) the method of getting on to the trampoline; (b) the first movement performed in a routine.

229

Open The coming out from a tucked or piked position for landing or for creating twists.

Orientate To find or correct one's mental condition in relation to the bed.

Out bounce A free bounce executed at the end of a competition routine to show the judges that the performer is under control.

Overthrow To go beyond the required, or normal, number of rotational degrees.

Piked A position where the body is bent at the hips only.

Pit model A trampoline set in the ground so that the top of the frame is level with the ground.

Porpus Forward somersault from Back Drop to Back Drop.

Portage To carry or transport.

Radius of gyration The distance from the centre of the rotation to the centre of the mass rotating about this point.

Randolph Forward somersault with two and a half twists. Also known as a Randy.

Rebound tumbling A term once used to denote the sport of trampolining.

Roller Seat Drop, full-twist to Seat Drop.

Roller stands The stands with swivel castors upon which the trampoline is transported.

Routine A series of movements linked together in swingtime.

Rudolph A forward somersault with one and a half twists. Also known as a Rudy.

Seat Drop A basic landing on the seat with the legs fully extended in front of the body.

Serolod A Ball-out with one and a half twists. (Named after Dolores Dixon because she performed this movement better than any other trampolinist.)

Sommy, Sommie Slang terms used for describing somersaults.

Spotter There are two meanings: (a) a person who stands ready to catch a performer; (b) a movement which takes off and lands on the same point.

Swingtime One movement performed immediately after another without a free bounce in between.

Swivel Hips Seat Drop, half-twist to Seat Drop.

Tramp Slang term for trampoline.

Transference of momentum Where the momentum from one part of the body is passed to the rest of the body. Also applied to transferring rotational momentum from a somersault to rotational momentum for a twist in twisting somersaults.

Travel Movement along the bed in the same direction in which the stunt is being performed.

Triffis Triple somersault with twist.

Triple Triple somersault.

Tuck A position where the body is flexed at the hips and the knees.

Turntable A Front Drop with lateral rotation of 360° to Front Drop. This is *not* a twisting movement but a side somersault performed in the horizontal plane.

Twister Slang term for a twisting somersault.

U.S.G.F. United States Gymnastic Federation.

Wrap A term used to describe the drawing-in of the arms for twisting movements.

15

Proficiency Awards of the British Trampoline Federation

This scheme was compiled by Peter Quinney and the author for the B.A.G.A. Trampoline Committee and was later adopted by the British Trampoline Federation on its formation in 1965

Rules and Regulations appertaining to Proficiency Awards

1. All applicants for each group must hold the previous award in that group, i.e. applicants for the Elementary Silver grade must hold the Elementary Bronze award.
2. Applicants for the Intermediate or Advanced groups must be up to the Gold standard of the preceding group, i.e. Intermediate applicants must be up to the Elementary Gold standard.
3. Where applicants do not already hold the Gold award of the preceding group, he or she will be asked to perform selected movements from this section to prove his or her worthiness to be examined. Should applicants fail to pass this test successfully, their request to continue at this juncture will be denied. The applicant must then qualify by taking the Bronze award of the preceding group, i.e. a person requesting to take the Intermediate Bronze award and failing to satisfy the examiner that he or she is up to this standard, must then take the elementary Bronze.

4. The examinations may be carried out by fully qualified coaches of the B.T.F. under the following conditions:

Elementary awards: Any qualified B.T.F. coach.

Intermediate awards: Any TWO qualified B.T.F. coaches *or* one B.T.F. advanced coach

Advanced awards: Any TWO B.T.F. advanced coaches. Any national grade coach is permitted to carry out these tests unassisted.

5. Successful candidates will be permitted to wear the proficiency badge of the appropriate standard and group at which they were tested and their names placed on the national register of trampolinists. Unsuccessful candidates will be told why they failed and will forfeit their application fee.

6. In every case the movements must be performed with good control and good form. Not more than TWO attempts may be made at stunts or routines. Examiners maintain the right to fail any performer who does not conform to the above requirements. Examiners may NOT assist in compiling the routines to be performed by the examinee.

ELEMENTARY BRONZE

Group A

Straight bounce.
Tuck Jump.
Piked Jump.
Straddle Jump.
Seat Drop.
Back Drop.
Knee Drop.
Hands-and-Knee Drop.
Front Drop.

Group B

Half turntable.
Hands and knees, forward turnover to seat.
Back Pull-over to hands and knees.

233

Back Drop to Front Drop.
Knee Drop forward turnover to back.

Group C

Seat Drop half-twist to feet.
Swivel Hips.
Back Drop half-twist to feet.
Half-twist to Front Drop.
Half-twist to Back Drop.

Requirements for a Pass

ALL movements from Group A.
Three movements from Group B.
Three movements from Group C.
One eight-bounce routine with not more than THREE moves
from each group.
Fold and unfold a trampoline with assistance.

ELEMENTARY SILVER

Group A

Swivel Hips.
Back Drop to Front Drop.
Front Drop (A, B & C).
Back Drop (A, B & C).
Flat back.
Crash dive.
Back Pull-over to feet.
Front Drop to Back Drop.
Half-turntable.

Group B

Three-quarter forward turnover to Seat Drop.
Tucked front somersault.
Tucked back somersault.
Three-quarter back somersault.

234

Crash dive forward turnover to front.
Knee Drop handstand, half-twist to knees.

Group C

Seat Drop half-twist to Front Drop.
Front Drop half-twist to Back Drop.
Front Drop half-twist to seat.
Cradle.
Full-twist to Back Drop.
Full-twist to Front Drop.
Seat Drop full-twist to Seat Drop.
Back Drop half-twist to Front Drop.

Requirements for a Pass

ALL movements from Group A.
Three movements from Group B.
Six movements from Group C.
Two eight-bounce routines to include not more than THREE moves from each group.
Candidates must hold Elementary Bronze.

ELEMENTARY GOLD

Group A

Full-twist jump.
One and three-quarter front somersault.
One and a quarter back somersault.
Barani.
Hollow-back somersault.
Crash dive forward turnover to back.
Back Drop Kaboom, back somersault to feet.
Cradle.
Full-twist to Front Drop.

Group B

Back Pull-over half-twist to Back Drop.
Corkscrew.
One and a half twist to Front Drop.

235

One and a half twist to Back Drop.
Full twisting front somersault to seat.
Half twisting three-quarter back somersault.

Group C

Crash dive to back—Corkscrew.
Barani—back somersault.
Knee Drop front somersault—Barani.
One and a quarter back somersault—Back Pull-over to feet.

Requirements for a Pass

ALL movements from Group A.
Four movements from Group B.
Two movements from Group C.
One eight-bounce routine to include any THREE movements from Group A, and one eight-bounce routine to include THREE movements from Group A, which must be different from those used in the first routine.
Candidates must hold Elementary Silver.

INTERMEDIATE BRONZE (WOMEN AND GIRLS)

Group A

Seat Drop full-twist to Seat Drop.
Back Drop full-twist to stand.
Front Drop half-twist to stand.
Full turntable.
Ball-out to seat.
Back Pull-over half-twist to Back Drop.

Group B

Front Cody to seat.
Cat-twist.
One and three-quarter somersault.
Hollow back somersault with half-twist.
Overturned Barani to back.
Piked back somersault.

236

Group C

  Overturned Barani to back—Back-Pull over to feet.
  Back Drop full-twist to feet—front somersault.
  Swivel Hips—Seat Drop full-twist to Seat Drop.
  One and three-quarter front somersault—half turntable.

Requirements for a Pass

  ALL movements from Group A.
  Four movements from Group B.
  Two movements from Group C.
  One eight-bounce routine containing FOUR movements from
  Group A.
  Fold and unfold a trampoline.
  Candidates must be up to Elementary Gold standard.

INTERMEDIATE SILVER (WOMEN AND GIRLS)

Group A

  Overthrown Barani.
  Piked back somersault.
  Cat-twist.
  Ball-out to feet.
  Three-quarter back somersault.
  One and a quarter somersault half-twist to Back Drop
  Front Cody to seat.
  Piked back somersault to seat.

Group B

  One and three-quarter front somersault.
  Hollow back somersault with half-twist.
  Back Cody.
  Front Cody to feet.
  Front somersault with full-twist to seat.
  Three-quarter turnover, half-twist to Front Drop.

Group C

  Crash dive—half-twist to Back Drop—Back Pull-over.

One and a quarter somersault, half-twist to Back Drop—
Back Pull-over.
Piked back somersault—Barani—piked back somersault.
Three-quarter back somersault—pull-over to back—pull-over
to feet.

Requirements for a Pass

ALL movements from Group A.
Four movements from Group B.
Two movements from Group C.
Two different eight-bounce routines, not to include jumps.
ALL stunts in the second routine to be different.
Candidates must hold the Intermediate Bronze.

INTERMEDIATE GOLD (WOMEN AND GIRLS)

Group A

Front Cody to feet.
Three-quarter forward turnover with half-twist to Front Drop.
Front somersault with full-twist to Seat Drop.
Corkscrew.
Hollow back somersault with half-twist.
Double front somersault to seat.
Back Drop vertical arch.
Back Drop *early* half-twist to Back Drop.

Group B

Three-quarter back somersault with half-twist to Back Drop.
Tucked back somersault with half-twist to feet.
One and three-quarter front somersault to Back Drop.
Back Cody.
Forward turnover with full-twist to Back Drop.
Ball-out Barani to hands and knees.

Group C

Double front somersault to Seat Drop—full-twist to Seat
Drop.
Front Cody to feet—Tucked Jump—back somersault.

238

Crash dive—early half-twist to Back Drop—Back Pull-over.
Tucked back somersault with half-twist to feet—forward
turnover to seat.

Requirements for a Pass

ALL movements from Group A.
Four movements from Group B.
Two movements from Group C.
Two different eight-bounce routines each containing one
different stunt from Group A and NO jumps.
Candidates must hold Intermediate Silver.

INTERMEDIATE BRONZE (MEN AND BOYS)

Group A

Seat Drop full-twist to Seat Drop (Roller).
Back Drop full-twist to stand.
Front Drop half-twist to stand.
Full turntable.
Back Pull-over half-twist to Back Drop.
Back Drop, Ball-out to seat.
Knee Drop front somersault.

Group B

Front Cody to seat.
Cat-twist.
One and three-quarter front somersault.
Hollow back somersault with half-twist.
Overturned Barani to Back.
Piked back somersault.

Group C

Overturned Barani—Back Pull-over to feet.
Back Drop full-twist to feet—front somersault.
Swivel Hips—Seat Drop full-twist to seat.
One and a quarter front somersault—half turntable.

PROFICIENCY AWARDS OF THE B.T.F.

Requirements for a Pass

ALL movements from Group A.

Four movements from Group B.

Two movements from Group C.

One eight-bounce routine containing FOUR movements from Group A.

Fold and unfold a trampoline.

Candidates must be up to the Elementary Gold standard.

INTERMEDIATE SILVER (MEN AND BOYS)

Group A

Front Cody to seat.

Cat-twist.

Front somersault with full-twist to seat.

Hollow back somersault half-twist to feet.

Overturned Barani to Back Drop.

Piked back somersault.

Ball-out to feet.

One and a quarter front somersault, half-twist to back

Group B

Front Cody to feet.

Back Cody.

Three-quarter back somersault with half-twist.

One and three-quarter front somersault.

Ball-out Barani to hands and knees.

Back somersault with full-twist.

Group C

Crash dive—half-twist to Back Drop—Back pull-over.

One and a quarter front somersault—Front Cody.

One and a quarter front somersault with half-twist to Back Drop—Back Pull-over.

Three-quarter back somersault—turnover to back—Back Pull-over.

PROFICIENCY AWARDS OF THE B.T.F.

Requirements for a Pass

ALL movements from Group A.
Four movements from Group B.
Two movements from Group C
Two different eight-bounce routines containing NO jumps.
(ALL stunts in the second routine must be different from the first.)
Candidates must hold the Intermediate Bronze.

INTERMEDIATE GOLD (MEN AND BOYS)

Group A

One and three-quarter front somersault to Back Drop.
Three-quarter back somersault with half-twist.
Front Cody to feet.
Corkscrew.
Crash dive, full-twist to Front Drop.
Back Drop, *early* half-twist to Back Drop.
Piked three-quarter back somersault.
Ball-out Barani to hands and knees.

Group B

Back somersault with full-twist.
One and a half twisting front somersault (Rudolph).
Back Drop, half-twist into back somersault.
One and a quarter back somersault half-twist to Front Drop.
Double somersault (front or back).
Side somersault.

Group C

One and three-quarter front somersault—Ball-out to feet.
One and three-quarter front somersault—half-twist to back somersault.
Corkscrew—Cat-twist.
Tucked back somersault—Barani—tucked back somersault.

Q 241

PROFICIENCY AWARDS OF THE B.T.F.

Requirements for a Pass

ALL movements from Group A.
Four movements from Group B.
Two movements from Group C.
Two different eight-bounce routines each containing one different stunt from Group A and no jumps.
Candidates must hold the Intermediate Silver.

ADVANCED BRONZE (WOMEN)

Group A

Back Cody.
Tucked back somersault with half-twist to feet.
Ball-out Barani to hands and knees.
Three-quarter back somersault with half-twist to Back Drop.
Back Drop, full-twist to Front Drop.
Back Drop Pull-over with half-twist to Back Drop.
One and three-quarter front somersault to Back Drop.
Piked three-quarter back somersault.

Group B

Back Drop Pull-over with half-twist to feet.
Front Cody, half-twist to Front Drop.
Back Drop, half-twist into back somersault (Baby Fliffus).
Crash dive, full-twist to Front Drop.
Back somersault with full-twist.
Ball-out Barani to feet.

Group C

Piked three-quarter back somersault—Back Cody.
Tucked back somersault with half-twist—front somersault.
One and three-quarter front somersault—Ball-out to feet.
One and a quarter back somersault—Back Drop Pull-over with half-twist to back.

Requirements for a Pass

ALL movements from Group A.
242

Four movements from Group B.
Two movements from Group C.
One eight-bounce routine to include at least THREE movements from Groups A and B.
Fold and unfold a trampoline.
Candidates must be up to Intermediate Gold standard.

ADVANCED SILVER (WOMEN)

Group A

Crash dive, full-twist to Front Drop.
Back Pull-over with half-twist to feet.
Front Cody with half-twist to Front Drop.
Back somersault with full-twist.
One and a quarter back somersault with half-twist to Front Drop.
Side somersault.
Ball-out Barani to feet.
One and three-quarter back somersault to hands and knees.

Group B

Three-quarter back somersault with full-twist to Front Drop.
One and a half twisting front somersault (Rudolph).
Crash dive, full twisting turnover to Back Drop.
Full twisting crash dive.
Any double somersault.
Half twisting Back Cody to back or seat.

Group C

Ball-out Barani to feet—back somersault.
One and three-quarter front somersault—Ball-out Barani to feet.
Tucked back somersault—full twisting back somersault.
Tucked back somersault with half-twist—Barani.

Requirements for a Pass

ALL movements from Group A.
Four movements from Group B.

243

Two movements from Group C.

Two different eight-bounce routines containing one different multiple somersault and one different full, or multiple, twisting somersault in each routine.

Candidates must hold the Advanced Bronze.

ADVANCED GOLD (WOMEN)

Group A

Three-quarter back somersault with full-twist to Front Drop.
One and a half twisting front somersault (Rudolph).
Any double somersault.
Baby Fliffus.
Crash dive, full-twist to Back Drop.
Half twisting Back Cody to back or seat.
One and three-quarter piked front somersault.
Piked Ball-out Barani to feet.

Group B

Fliffus.
Half twisting Back Cody to feet.
Back somersault with double twist.
Piked Back Cody to feet.
Piked Baby Fliffus.
One and three-quarter somersault to Back Drop, Corkscrew.

Group C

Three-quarter back somersault with full-twist—Back Cody.
Tucked back somersault—Rudolph.
One and three-quarter piked front somersault—Ball-out to feet.
Piked Ball-out Barani to feet—back somersault.

Requirements for a Pass

ALL movements from Group A.
Four movements from Group B.
Two movements from Group C.
Two different eight-bounce routines containing one multiple

244

somersault and one multiple twisting movement in each routine.

Candidates must hold the Advanced Silver.

ADVANCED BRONZE (MEN)

Group A

Back Cody.
Front Cody half-twist to Front Drop.
Side somersault.
Piked one and a quarter back somersault.
One and a quarter back somersault half-twist to Front Drop.
Back Drop, half-twist into back somersault.
Ball-out Barani to feet.
Inverted arch.

Group B

Three-quarter back somersault with full-twist to Front Drop.
Back Cody with half-twist.
Back somersault with full-twist.
Front Cody with half-twist to feet.
One and a half twisting front somersault (Rudolph).
One and three-quarter back somersault.

Group C

Piked three-quarter back somersault—Back Cody.
Piked back somersault to seat—full-twist to seat.
Crash dive—half-twist into back somersault.
One and three-quarter somersault—Ball-out Barani to feet.

Requirements for a Pass

ALL movements from Group A.
Four movements from Group B.
Two movements from Group C.
One eight-bounce routine to include any THREE moves from Groups A and B.
Fold and unfold a trampoline.
Candidates must be up to Intermediate Gold standard.

ADVANCED SILVER (MEN)

Group A

Any double somersault.
Back somersault with full-twist.
One and a half twisting front somersault (Rudolph).
Crash dive, half-twist into back somersault.
Back Cody half-twist to seat.
Ball-out full-twist to Back Drop.
Three-quarter back somersault with full-twist.
One and three-quarter front somersault.

Group B

Any fliffus.
Back Cody half-twist to feet.
Back somersault with double twist.
Back Cody with full-twist.
Piked Back Cody.
Piked Baby Fliffus.

Group C

One and a half twisting front somersault—back somersault with full-twist.
Piked one and three-quarter somersault—Ball-out with full-twist to Back Drop.
Three-quarter somersault with full-twist—Back Cody.

Requirements for a Pass

ALL movements from Group A.
Four movements from Group B.
One movement from Group C.
Two different eight-bounce routines to include ONE multiple somersault and ONE multiple twisting somersault in each.
Candidates must hold the Advanced Bronze.

246

ADVANCED GOLD (MEN)

Group A

Any fliffus.
Double back somersault.
Back somersault with double-twist.
Full twisting crash dive.
One and three-quarter back somersault half-twist to Back Drop.
Back Cody half-twist to feet.
Piked Baby fliffus.
Piked Back Cody.

Group B

Two and a half twisting front somersault (Randolph).
Back somersault with triple twist.
Full twisting Back Cody.
Two and three-quarter front somersault.
Double front somersault with full-twist to seat.
Double Back Cody.
Piked double somersault.

Group C

One and three-quarter back somersault—back Cody.
Double back somersault—Barani.
Fliffus—back somersault.

Requirements for a Pass

ALL movements from Group A.
Four movements from Group B.
One movement from Group C.
Two different eight-bounce routines each to contain:
One fliffus.
One multiple twisting somersault.
One cody.
Candidates must hold Advanced Silver.

247

16

Coaching Awards of the British Trampoline Federation

This scheme was compiled by Peter Quinney and the author for the B.A.G.A. Trampoline Committee and was later adopted by the British Trampoline Federation on its formation in 1965

The Coaching Award Scheme provides for three classes of coach: Coach, Advanced Coach, National Grade Coach.

Qualifications for the Coaching Awards

Applicants for the advanced coaching certificate must possess the preliminary coaching certificate, subject to the Central Council reserving the right to waive this rule at its discretion.

Only fully paid-up members of the British Trampoline Federation are eligible to be examined.

Syllabus for the Coach's Award

Candidates will be required to take a written examination on the mechanical principles involved in trampolining and the techniques used in performing the movements set out on the personal check-off list. They will also be required to teach and coach any individual movements selected by the examiner from the movements referred to above.

The written examination will cover the following topics:
1. Knowledge of trampolining terms.
2. With reference to trampolining, explain and give examples of:

COACHING AWARDS OF THE B.T.F.

(a) Action and reaction (Newton's third Law of Motion).
(b) Angular velocity.
(c) Transference of momentum.
3. Safety precautions:
(a) Prior to the use of the trampoline.
(b) Safety to the performer during use.
(c) After use of the trampoline.
(d) Portaging.
4. Give the advantages and disadvantages of the different types of equipment.
5. Outline the programme for a trampolining class.
6. List the progressions you would use to teach the movements selected by the examiner.
7. List the aids available for teaching trampolining.
8. Devise two eight-bounce routines so that the stunts selected lead one into the other and flow smoothly.
9. True or false questions.
Candidates must score at least 50 per cent of the marks awarded for each question and 60 per cent of the total marks.

Syllabus for the Advanced Coaching Award

Candidates will be required to take a written examination on the mechanics involved in trampolining and the techniques used in performing all the movements set out on the advanced check-off list. They will also be required to teach and coach any individual movements selected by the examiner from the movements referred to above.

The syllabus for the written examination will cover the following:
1. Knowledge of advanced trampolining terms.
2. Newton's Laws of Motion with reference to trampolining.
3. Explain the principles of twisting.
4. Give details of the mechanical aids used in trampolining.
5. Explain the mechanical principles of rotation.
6. Lesson planning.
7. Show the progressions you would use to perform certain movements together in swingtime as selected by the examiner.

249

8. Detail the methods you would use in the teaching of certain advanced movements as selected by the examiner.

9. Devise two ten-bounce routines to include multiple somersault and twisting movements so that the stunts selected lead one into the other and flow smoothly.

Candidates must score at least 50 per cent of the marks awarded for each question and 75 per cent of the total marks.

National Grade Coach

This title is awarded to qualified advanced coaches who, in the opinion of the Central Council of the B.T.F., have proved themselves to be worthy of such distinction.

Acknowledgements

The author acknowledges with thanks the help given by Sister Aloysius, Ted Blake, the British Amateur Gymnastic Association, the British Trampoline Federation, Lynn Davies, Ralph. Diapher, Bill Dodds, Dick Graham, Bill Ludgrove, Robert Mealey, George Nissen, Wally Orner, Pat Winkle, and his wife

Index

INDEX